The Architecture of Wine

Die Architektur des Weines

L'architecture du vin

The Architecture of Wine
Bordeaux and Napa Valley

Die Architektur des Weines
im Bordeaux und im Napa Valley

L'architecture du vin
dans le Bordelais et à Napa Valley

Dirk Meyhöfer & Olaf Gollnek
with an essay by
Peter C. Hubschmid

GINGKO PRESS
Corte Madera 2000

Inhalt · Contents · Sommaire

Die Architektur des Weines
Anmerkungen zu einem neuen alten Bautypus

Dirk Meyhöfer

So wundervoll archaisch und kulturtragend das Thema Wein ist, so neu und überraschend, fast exotisch mag es auf den ersten Blick erscheinen, in der Architektur für den Wein ein avantgardistisches Thema sehen zu wollen. Weingüter, in der Regel früher Weinbauernhöfe, gibt es seit über 2000 Jahren. Eine präzise Architekturdebatte über einen solchen Bautypus, so wie sie über eine Kathedrale, einen Bahnhof oder ein Bankgebäude geführt werden kann, konnte es so lange nicht geben, wie es sich im wesentlichen um Spielarten eines Bauernhofes oder Gutes mit einem Herrenhaus (im Französischen „Château") und Nebengebäuden handelte. Und dennoch konnte schon sehr wohl eine Art „Geschichte der Architektur im Weinbau" geschrieben werden, in der der Satz zu finden ist: „Die Architektur im Weinbau (von Bordeaux) muß also die Gesamtheit der Baulichkeiten eines Weinguts berücksichtigen, wobei es nichts Unmotiviertes gibt".[1] Wir kommen darauf zurück, aber zu beginnen ist dann doch eher mit dem Ende und jenem Ereignis, das, wenn schon nicht zur Entdeckung, dann aber ganz bestimmt zur Wiederentdeckung des Themas führte: 1988 veranstaltete das renommierte und bezogen auf Architektur und Design avantgardistische „Centre Pompidou" eine große Ausstellung über die „Châteaux Bordeaux". Das war der Durchbruch.

Jean Dethier, belgischer Architekt mit Wohnsitz in Paris und Ausstellungsmacher mit einer Spürnase für brisante Architekturthemen, sollte in den achtziger Jahren eine Architekturkolumne für das führende Weinmagazin im Bordeaux „L'Amateur de Bordeaux" schreiben. Er erkannte sehr schnell, daß die „wichtigste Kunst, die in einzigartiger Synthese zu fördern sich die Weinbaugesellschaft von Bordeaux entschlossen hat, die Architektur ist".[2]

In der Praxis bedeutete das: Den Winzern im Bordelais war es schon im frühen 19. Jahrhundert gelungen, einen Begriff mit aristokratischem Klang zum Markenzeichen zu machen: das Château. Sie stellten die unterschwellige Assoziation her, daß der Wein immer kongenial zu einer prächtigen Schloßarchitektur sei. Auch wenn die Konsumenten dies inzwischen weltweit glauben mögen, sagt die Bezeichnung „Château" über die Architekturqualität des jeweiligen dazu gehörigen Weinbauernhofes – denn mehr ist es ja eigentlich nicht – wenig aus. Mehrere tausend Châteaux mag es heute noch im Bordelais geben, dazu zählen solche wie das stolze Château Margaux, wo der Geist der Antike zu wohnen scheint, andere hingegen besitzen nicht einmal die Ausstrahlung eines durchschnittlichen Bauernhauses, weil ihre Bauweise zu schematisch und trivial erscheint. Doch alle profitieren von der Legende, die Dethier als ein frühes perfektes Beispiel einer imposanten Corporate Identity, in diesem Fall der Corporate Architecture, sieht.

Was ist eigentlich ein Weinbauernhof?

Seit Jahrhunderten besteht das Weingut generell aus vier Teilen, die erst ein Ganzes ausmachen: „Château", „Chai", „Cuvier" und dem eigentlichen Weinberg. Im „Cuvier" (dem Gärkeller) stehen die großen, heute meist stählernen zylindrischen „Cuves", in denen der Wein gärt, im „Chai" (dem Lagerkeller) ruhen die „Barriques". Das sind handgemachte Eichenfässer mit etwa 225 Litern Inhalt, in denen der Wein nach dem Gärprozeß mindestens zwei Jahre lang ruht und reift, bevor er auf Flaschen gezogen wird (vgl. a. Peter C. Hubschmid: „Das Handwerk des Weinmachens"; ab S. 208).

Es ist nicht zu bestreiten, daß die Weinerzeugung im Bordelais bis auf römische Zeiten zurückgeht. Im großen Stil begann man jedoch erst zum Ende des 17. Jahrhundert, also im Vergleich zu anderen Weinbaugebieten sehr spät, die angeschwemmten Kiesböden des feuchtwarmen und salzhaltigen Ozeanklimas an der Gironde/Garonne für den Weinanbau zu kultivieren. Zwischen 1840 und 1870 erlebten die großen Weingüter an der Gironde-Mündung dann ihre erste Blütezeit, gerade als in der Architektur üppige Stilvielfalt Mode wurde. Keine Überraschung also, wenn der Streifzug durch das Médoc zum Abenteuerspaziergang durch die Architekturgeschichte wird. Ägypter, Griechen, Goten, Palladio, Renaissance, Barock und immer wieder Klassik – wer zählt die Vorbilder, wer untersucht die eklektischen Verbindungen? Manchmal wirkt es so, als sollte die gesamte Stilvielfalt von Orient und Okzident an einem einzigen Château demonstriert werden.

Das Château Cos d´Estournel aus dem Jahr 1830 ist ein solcher Fall (vgl. auch S. 38ff), ein Ort wie aus einer Fata Morgana: In jedem Augenblick könnten Elefanten oder Kamele hier auftreten ohne aufzufallen, so phantasievoll orientalisch sind die mit grazilen Türmchen geschmückten Hallen, die nördlich von Pauillac und dem Gut Lafite-Rothschild oberhalb einer Straßenkurve ganz plötzlich aus den grünen Weingärten auftauchen: Beide Güter (Lafite-Rothschild und Cos d´Estournel) haben übrigens bravourös eine etwa hundertjährige Phase des Leidens überstanden, die erst seit etwa 30 Jahren beendet ist, in der Reblaus und Mehltau, Wirtschaftskrisen und Kriege die Winzer im Bordelais immer wieder in solche Existenznöte gebracht haben, die heute, da Grand Cru-Weine an der Börse fast zu einer Art Ersatzwährung gereift sind, unvorstellbar sind.

Erst seit den sechziger Jahren mit einer kleinen Pause zu Zeiten der Ölpreiskrisen in den frühen siebziger Jahren geht es wieder so rasant aufwärts, daß man zu Investitionen im großen Stil neigt. Erst jetzt kann man wieder an die großen Architekturtraditionen des 19. Jahrhunderts anschließen.

Doch bedurfte es eines genialen Kuriers wie Jean Dethier, der zwischen alter und neuer Welt querdachte, und eines neureichen, quicklebendigen Herausforderers. In diesem Fall sozusagen der uneheliche Sohn des Vaters, der – soviel sei verraten – inzwischen liebevoll adoptiert worden ist.

Von Bordeaux nach Napa Valley

Jetzt kommt nämlich Kalifornien ins Spiel, mit seinem lieb-
lichen Napa Valley, das eine Stunde nördlich von San Francisco liegt: „A veritable garden of Eden", wie der Heraus-
geber des Gastro-Journals „Pacific Epicure",[3] John Doeper,
in gefälliger Selbstbetrachtung schreibt, ein farbenfreudiges
Patchwork aus Provence, Toscana, Bordeaux, Champagne
und Rheingau, mit einer Sonne wie in Mexiko und dem
strengen, Regen bringenden Pazifikwind mit gewaltigen
Wettern, Himmeln und Weinen.

Noch in den sechziger Jahren war Wein aus Napa Valley
in Frankreich nicht ernst genommen worden, Baron Philippe
de Rothschild hielt ihn als „überwürztes Industriegesöff für
nicht weltmarktfähig".[4] Und er stand mit dieser Meinung
nicht allein da.

Das Napa Valley hatte einen ähnlich einschneidenden
Karriereknick hinter sich wie das Bordelais. In Kalifornien
wurde seit etwa 1839 Wein angebaut, vorwiegend „Gewürz-
traminer" von deutschen Winzern, bis Reblaus, Krieg und
zusätzlich ziemlich radikal die Prohibition in den dreißiger
Jahren fast alles auf Null fuhr: Es überlebten 24 Weingüter,
wo heute wieder 300 sind. Und die teilweise nur deswegen,
weil sie den Meßwein für die Kirchen produzieren durften.

Aufstieg und Wiederentdeckung war energiegeladenen
Promotern wie Robert Mondavi zu verdanken, der ab 1966
generalistisch, gründlich und mit einem Marketing, als wollte er einen Porsche verkaufen, ans Werk ging. Oder einem
Mann wie Peter Newton mit den Sterling Vineyards, 1972,
einer perfekten Inszenierung, auf einem Hügel mit einem
Talblick, der Gänsehaut erzeugt. Das Weingut steht auf einer
Hügelkuppe und verbirgt sich hinter der Kulisse eines weißen „kykladischen" Klosters. Das Bauensemble war den Besuchern von vornherein bekannt, weil es die Weinetiketten
schmückte, eine geschickte Corporate Identity Maßnahme,
die den Weingutsbesitzern auf den französischen Châteaux
abgeschaut war. Innen dürfen die Besucher in einer Self
Guided Tour alle Stufen des Making of Wine erleben: das
erste „Museum des Weines" auf der Welt mit riesigen Besucherzahlen (vgl. a. S. 128ff).

Robert Mondavi zieht das Motiv seines Weingutes mit
einem erdverwachsenen Turm und einem brückenschlagen-
den Empfangsgebäude ebenso perfekt bis zum Briefkopf und
den Weinetiketten durch, und er verbindet seinen Wein mit
heiteren Vernissagen und Sommerfesten im schattigen In-
nenhof und auf dem grünen Rasen seines Anwesens: „Wein
und Kultur gehören zusammen, Wein ist nicht wie Whisky,
Wein ist kein alkoholhaltiger Drink. Wein ist Kunst. Wein ist
Leben!" würdigte die „Zeit" das grundsätzliche Credo der
Napa-Winzer.[5]

Vom Weinbauernhof zur Weinfabrik

Nur wer genau hinschaut, sieht neben dem Turm der Mondavi Winery, daß hinter hohen Mauern und grünen Anpflanzungen eine gar nicht so kleine Weinfabrik steht. Im Napa Valley geht es eben nicht nur um einen intimen Weinbauernhof. Zu Gärkeller, Tanklager, Keller, Lager, treten Show- und Tasting Room, Shop, Vip- und Barbecue Area, manchmal sogar Musikraum und Weinbibliothek; zusammen eine der komplexesten Bauaufgaben der Welt, weil die Amerikaner wie Industriebarone ans Weinmachen herangehen und alle Register des Marketings ziehen, wenn in Europa immer noch mehr das Handwerk gefragt ist (vgl. a. S. 116ff).

Sterling und Mondavi überraschten alle, weil bis dato die Güter entweder wie die „Villa Hadrian oder die Ponderosa"[6] (Architekturkritiker Raymond Ryan) aussahen. Mit nicht immer sicherem Stilwillen wurden die europäischen Vorbilder als Kulissenarchitektur verwendet oder man bekannte sich einfach zu den Ursprüngen.

Es waren dann diese neuen kalifornischen Vorbilder, vor allem das durchaus aggressive Marketing, die in den achtziger Jahren die Winzer in Frankreich aus ihrem Dornröschenschlaf aufweckten. Jean Dethier, der inzwischen Napa Valley bereist hatte, übernahm die Rolle des wachküssenden Prinzen. Es wurde auch Zeit für neue Konzepte. Inzwischen war die Kulturlandschaft des Bordelais bedroht. Die Landschaft wurde zersiedelt, gesichtslose Neu- und Anbauten verstellten den Blick auf alte Châteaux. Die Gefahr des Identitätsverlustes war gegeben, wenn der große Wein nicht mehr auf dem Château, sondern in der Kulisse von Allerweltsarchitektur reifen würde.

Wettbewerbe verändern das Denken und die Landschaft

Gleich mehrere Ereignisse führten dann in der zweiten Hälfte der achtziger Jahre in Frankreich dazu, daß man tatsächlich im Bordeaux von Napa lernte und den Trend brechen konnte. Vor allem der Initialzündung durch die Ausstellung im Centre Pompidou war dies zu verdanken, als sechs internationale Architektengruppen (Jeremy und Fenella Dixon mit Mark Pimlott; Florence Lipsky und Pascal Rollet und Vincent Defos du Rau; Fernando Montes; Bertrand Nivelle; Bruno Reichlin; Charles Vanderhove) ihren neuen „Idealtypus" eines Château vorstellen konnten. Die Entwürfe für einen imaginären Standort erinnerten an Ritterburgen, Flußschiffe oder ein Stückchen Revolutionsarchitektur von 1789. Manchmal lagen Gestalt und Dekor zwar an der Grenze zur übertriebenen Disneyland-Architektur, sie bewiesen aber glasklar, daß man die Bauaufgabe „Château" mit Phantasie angreifen kann.

Ein anderer Wettbewerb wurde hingegen realisiert. Auch er war damals im Centre Pompidou präsentiert worden. Im Weinbaugebiet Duhart-Millon fehlten dem dortigen Château Pichon-Longueville, einem klar gegliederten und hochgereckten Schloß, wie es auch an der Loire stehen könnte, Lagerkeller und Göranlagen. Im August 1988 gewannen die beiden Pariser Architekten Patrick Dillon und Jean de

Gastines (gegen die beiden Spanier Alberto Ustarroz / Manuel Iniguez und den Pariser Fernando Montes) den Wettbewerb. Schon das Wettbewerbsprogramm (vgl. a. S. 68) kündigte eine neue Dimension für ein Château Bordeaux an: Der wachsende Tourismus fordert inzwischen seinen Tribut, und deswegen bekommen Château, Chai und Cuvier Konkurrenz: Verkaufspavillon, ein kleines Museum, Parkplätze, ein „Theater des Weines". Man hat gelernt: Jean Michel Cazes, der Hausherr auf Pichon-Longueville und inzwischen einer der wesentlichen Promotoren der neuen Weinarchitektur-Kultur im Bordelais, sagte damals: „Ich will ein klassisches Weinschloß für das dritte Jahrtausend!" Er hat es bekommen: axial und symmetrisch, mit Obelisken, Bögen und Veduten. Ein Spektakel, zwar aus Beton, das aber nach nur 10 Jahren von Weinranken und durch würdige Alterung in den Status des „Schon-Ewig-Dazu-Gehörenden" versetzt wurde.

Branding und Corporate Architecture

Zwei andere Schlösser haben ebenfalls den Boden für einen neuen Aufbruch bestellt. Für den Wiederaufbau des Château d'Arsac, einem Weingut in der Nähe von Margeaux, wählten Philippe und Francoise Raoux inmitten all der etablierten Weingüter eine Strategie, die auf die verkaufsfördernde Wirkung von auffälliger Architektur, im Detail heißt das, kräftiger blauer Farbe, setzte (vgl. a. S. 94ff).

Der Baron Philippe Rothschild hatte sich schon in den zwanziger Jahren durch ein eigenes Weinbau-Museum auf seinem Gut Mouton ein Denkmal gesetzt und beschäftigte schon damals Charles Siclis, einen Theaterarchitekten aus Paris, zu Dekorationszwecken. Cousin Eric de Rothschild ließ dann in den achtziger Jahren auf dem Nachbargut Lafite den postmodernen Komödianten Richardo Bofill einen neuen Chai, „den besonders symbolischen Teils eines Châteaus – des am meisten in Ehren gehaltenen Bereiches"[7] (Jean Dethier) bauen. Dieser wurde wegen seines inneren kreisrunden Säulenringes von vielen Besuchern als sehr theatralisch empfunden, Baron de Rothschild sieht hingegen „eine Mystik, die gewissermaßen räumlicher Ausdruck unserer ethischen Vorstellungen von Wein ist".[8]

Der Baron stellte aber auch fest, daß eine „kreisförmige Ausrichtung und damit zentral ausgerichtete Anordnung den Vorteil der Einsparung von Arbeitskräften hat". Weil der Wein eben viermal im Jahr umgelagert werden muß, und so über den Daumen Einsparungen von 300 Kilometern ergeben!

Die Botschaft hinter dieser Aussage ist einfach: Es geht eben nicht nur um Theatralik, Symbolik und Schönheit, sondern immer auch um Funktionalität und Zweckmäßigkeit. Um die optimale Umsetzung des neuen alten Bautypus „Château", dem Weinbauernhof, der inzwischen zur Weinfabrik mit öffentlichem Marketingareal gereift ist. Es geht eben nicht nur um Stil und Ästhetik.

Eine neue Architektur des Weines

Zwischenzeitlich entstand im Napa Tal ein opulentes Freilichtmuseum der Architektur, das doch ein amüsantes Studium der verschiedenen Stile und Moden aus den letzten 30 bis 40 Jahren mit dem Ergebnis zuläßt, daß bei der hier erreichten Qualität Stil wirklich nur noch Geschmackssache ist. Irgendwie überzeugen die meisten Weingüter durch eine sympathische Kultiviertheit und eine zentrale Entwurfsidee (s. a. Porträts der Weingüter). Die aussagekräftigsten und auch unterschiedlichsten Prototypen einer neuen Ära gebaut zu haben – diese Ehre gehört zweifelsohne den Amerikanern in Napa Valley. Die Gründe mögen darin liegen, daß viel frisches Kapital in den Westen fließt. Plötzlich gilt es als fein, in Wein zu investieren. Zweitens verhindern keine verkrusteten Klischees und Traditionen architektonische Visionen. Hier ist alles möglich. Drittens wirkten die hedonistischen Zeiten der achtziger Jahre wie ein Treibhaus für Ideen.

Der Stil in Napa heißt „bester Pluralismus"! Hier steht das „postmoderne" Clos Pegase neben Dominus Estate der Puristen Herzog und de Meuron. Hinzu kommen Modernisierungen und Rekonstruktionen von Bauten aus dem letzten Jahrhundert (Beringer, Coppola, Far Niente). Was Jean Dethier aber befürchtet hatte, daß „das Schlimmste neben dem Besten zu finden ist",[9] hat sich nicht bewahrheitet. Der Einfluß der Crazy People wie Walt Disneys Witwe, dem Regisseur Francis Ford Coppola, Bob Sinkskey, der begehrte Dinner-Parties in seinen Wein-Katakomben veranstaltet, sorgte für Qualität und eine wahrhafte Aufbruchsstimmung.

Die wichtigste Ansage, für eine architektonische Entwicklung ist aber die, wie in Gegenwart und Zukunft auf dem Lande gebaut werden kann und ein neues Verständnis einer Symbiose aus Natur und Kultur entstehen könnte. Es gilt, Ressourcen zu schonen – selbst im weniger dicht besiedelten Nordkalifornien. Und es gilt, große Baumassen zu integrieren: Gewerbe- und Kulturbauten, Show- und Arbeitsbereiche. Wenn möglich, verstecken sich die Bauten in der Landschaft. Beispielsweise als Tunnel unter der Erde, was dem Wein gut tut und inzwischen dazu geführt hat, daß nirgendwo auf der Erde Tunnelbaufirmen so lukrativ zu betreiben sind wie in Kalifornien.

Zum andern werden Topografie und Rasen zu Helfern bei der Fassadengestaltung. Prominentes Beispiel ist die amerikanische Dependence des königlich-spanischen Hoflieferanten Artesa, die sich von oben in eine Hügelpyramide eingräbt. Die Bauten von Opus One schließlich landen wie ein Ufo auf einer Rasenkuppe. Hier im Napa Valley ist die Grenze zwischen Architektur, Landscaping und Landart fließend.

Und noch eines fällt auf: Opus One wirkt wie eine Synthese aus europäischer und amerikanischer Baukultur, wenn ein Baukörper aus schwerem Gestein auf eine amerikanische Dachveranda aus silbern glänzendem Holz trifft. Welche Bauaufgabe wäre dafür geeigneter als eine Architektur für den Wein, wo sich Lebenskunst, Klima, Kultur, Architektur und Wein vermischen – Napa als Global-Vineyard!

Im Médoc ist man nicht ganz so weit gegangen, vielleicht hat man es auch gar nicht nötig. Die Weinpreise dort schreiben allemal und immer wieder locker eine Null mehr auf das Papier. Die Weingüter sind dort (noch) kein touristisches Ereignis wie in Napa, wo ein eigener Eisenbahnzug durchs Tal stampft und die Weingüter spezielle Barbecuezonen vorhalten. In Frankreich führt man kein offenes Haus, statt dessen läuft alles nach diskreter Voranmeldung.

Und das hatte zur Folge, daß sich die Architekten außen zurück gehalten haben und zum Gralshüter der Tradition wurden. Explosive Raumwunder gibt es innen zu besichtigen. Exklusives Beispiel ist Ricardo Bofills Weinkellerrotunde für Lafite-Rothschild. Außen ist dieses Weingut nach wie vor ein liebliches Abbild eines französischen Landidylls.

Selbst das architektonische Vorzeigeprojekt Pichon-Longueville vermeidet nach außen zu starke Avancen an die Architektur des 20. Jahrhunderts. So halten es auch die Châteaux Léoville-Poyferré und Branaire und werden zu Beispielen für behutsamen Weiterbau im Bestand. Der Neubau der Domaines Henry Martin respektiert die belanglosen Vorgaben einer Dorfstraße. Nein. Keines der Beispiele aus dem Médoc will Architekturgeschichte so richtig weiterschreiben.

Das wollen die Franzosen dann lieber gleich in Kalifornien. Wie mit „Dominus" in Yountville, bei dem französische Prominenz wie Christian Moueix, der Direktor des berühmten Château Petrus in Pomerol, beteiligt ist. Er hat mit den Schweizer Avantgarde-Architekten Herzog und de Meuron hier ganz bestimmt Architekturgeschichte schreiben können.

Dominus ist alles: Vergangenheit, Gegenwart und Zukunft. Eine Steinmauer wird zur Hülle für einen „archaischen Container", in dem alle Belange einer „Winery" untergebracht sind. Dominus verrät nicht die Wurzeln des Weinbaus, kommt sozusagen „down to earth". Es ist im Innern modern, wie ein Labor, voller Überraschungen und Erlebnisse – ein großer Wurf eben.

Die „Reduktionisten" und sensiblen Wahrnehmungsartisten Herzog und de Meuron haben sich mit diesem Gebäude in die Liste der Ewig-Besten-Architekten des 20. Jahrhunderts eingetragen und sie haben einen neuen Prototypen eines Château geschaffen. Wir sind gespannt, wie es im nächsten Jahrtausend weitergeht.

1 Robert Coustet: „Geschichte der Architektur im Weinbau" in: „Châteaux Bordeaux", Bern 1989, S. 63

2 Châteaux Bordeaux – Baukunst und Weinbau, The German Museum of Architecture, Bern 1989

3 John Doerper: Wine Country, California´s Napa & Sonoma Valleys, S. 12ff, Oakland, 1998

4 Sibylle Zehle: Herzblut und roter Wein in „Die Zeit" No. 6/99

5 ebd.

6 Raymond Ryan in Baumeister 7/98 pp. 36ff

7 Châteaux Bordeaux, S. 173

8 ebd.

9 ebd. S. 180

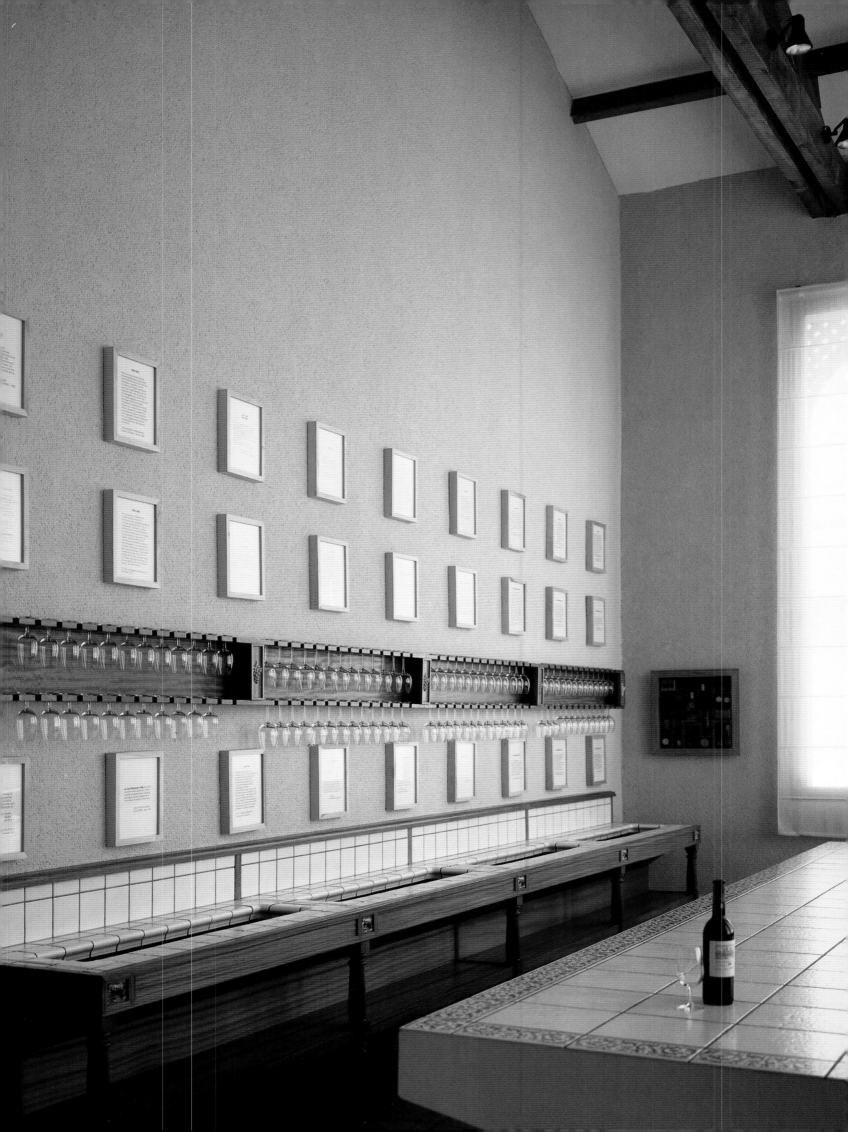

The Architecture of Wine
Notes on a New, Old Type of Architecture

Dirk Meyhöfer

As wonderfully archaic, cultural, new and surprising the subject of wine may be, the desire to perceive an avant-garde theme in the architecture of wine may well seem almost exotic at first. Wine-growing estates, formerly wine-growing "farms" as a rule, have existed for over 2000 years. Whilst ever such a variety of farms or estates with a manor house ("chateau" in French) and annexes existed, it was impossible to hold a precise, architectural debate on this type of architecture, as was the case with a cathedral, station or bank. Nevertheless, a kind of "history of architecture in viniculture" was able to be written in which the following sentence can be found: "The architecture of (Bordeaux's) viniculture therefore has to take all the buildings of an estate into consideration, whereby nothing is unmotivated"[1]. We will come back to this point, but I would rather begin with the end and with the event that led, if not to the discovery, then most definitely to the rediscovery of the subject: in 1988 the renowned – and, in terms of architecture and design, avant-garde -"Centre Pompidou" organised a great exhibition on the "chateaux of Bordeaux". This was the breakthrough.

In the eighties Jean Dethier, a Belgian architect living in Paris, also an exhibition organiser with a nose for explosive architectural subjects, was to write a column on architecture for the leading wine magazine "L'Amateur de Bordeaux". He quickly recognised that "the most important art that the Bordeaux society of viniculture has decided to promote, in a unique act of union, is that of architecture"[2].

This meant, in practise, that the wine-growers of Bordeaux had already succeeded in the early 19th century in turning the aristocratic sounding term "chateau" into a trademark. They created the subliminal association that the wine always befitted the magnificent architecture of a chateau. Even if, in the meantime, consumers world-wide may wish to believe this, the term "chateau" says very little about the architectural quality of the respective wine-growing farm – for it really is no more than this – belonging to it. There are perhaps still thousands of chateaux in Bordeaux today, including ones like the impressive Chateau Margeaux where the spirit of antiquity appears to live on; others, however, do not even possess the aura of an average farmhouse, their style of construction appearing too schematised and trivial. And yet everyone profits from the legend that Dethier sees as a perfect, early example of an imposing corporate identity, in this case of corporate architecture.

What Exactly is a Wine-Growing Farm?

In earlier centuries the wine-growing estate was generally made up of four parts making a whole: the "chateau", "chai", "cuvier" and the actual vineyard itself. The large, nowadays mostly steel cylindrical "cuves" in which the wine ferments lie in the "cuvier" (the fermentation cellar); the "barriques" lie in the "chai" (the storage cellar). The barriques are hand-made oak barrels, with a capacity of approximately 225 li-tres, in which the wine rests and matures for a period of at least 2 years after the fermentation process before being bot-tled (cf. also Peter C. Hubschmid, The Art of Winemaking; pp. 214 ff).

The fact that wine production in Bordeaux dates back to Roman times is beyond doubt. However, it wasn't until the end of the 17th century, very late in fact compared with other wine-growing regions, that the large-scale cultivation of the alluvial gravel soils of the humid, salty ocean climate on the Gironde/Garonne for wine-growing purposes really began. The great estates on the Gironde estuary first flour-ished between 1840 and 1870, in the exact same period that a luxurious variety of styles became fashionable in architec-ture. It therefore comes as no surprise when an expedition through the Medoc turns into an adventure trail through architectural history. Egyptians, Greeks, Goths, Palladio. Re-naissance, Baroque and, time and again, classical – who counts the examples, who investigates the eclectic connec-tions? Sometimes it appears as if every variation in style from the Orient and Occident are demonstrated in a single chateau.

The Chateau Cos d'Estournel from the year 1830 – a mir-age-like apparition – is representative of this (see also pp. 38 ff). So elaborately oriental are the halls adorned with slender turrets, which spring up quite suddenly out of the green vineyard to the north of Paulliac and the Lafite-Rothschild estate above a curve in the road, that elephants or camels could make an entrance here at any moment without ap-pearing out of place. Incidentally, both estates (Lafite-Roth-schild and Cos d'Estournel) resiliently survived almost a cen-tury of suffering – ending around 30 years ago – in which phylloxera and mildew coupled with economic crises and wars repeatedly led to struggles for existence amongst the wine-growers of Bordeaux. Such struggles would be un-imaginable today now that Grand Cru wines are matured almost as a kind of alternative currency on the stock ex-change.

It wasn't until the sixties, with a short break at the time of the oil price crisis in the early seventies, that things start-ed to improve dramatically, creating a tendency amongst investors to invest heavily. Only now did the possibility re-emerge for us to follow the architectural traditions of the 19th century.

However, it took a messenger as brilliant as Jean Dethier, a lateral thinker between old and new wine, and a nouveau-riche, vivacious challenger; in this case, as it were, the father's illegitimate son who – this much we know- has since been lovingly adopted.

From Bordeaux to the Napa Valley

Now we will bring California into the picture, with its charming Napa Valley situated one hour north of San Francisco: "A veritable garden of Eden", as John Doeper, editor of the gastronomy journal "Pacific Epicure"[3] wrote in a pleasing self-observation: a colourful patchwork of the Provence, Tuscany, Bordeaux, Champagne and Rhine region with the sun of Mexico and the strong Pacific wind bringing in the rain, and with its powerful weather, skies and wine.

In the sixties wine from the Napa Valley was still not taken seriously in France. Baron Philippe de Rothschild considered it to be "over-spiced industrial swill (which was) not marketable internationally"[4]. And he was not alone in his opinion.

The Napa Valley has also undergone a drastic career turn similar to that of Bordeaux. In California wine had been cultivated since 1839, primarily "Gewurztraminer" by German wine-growers. It was all reduced to nothing by phylloxera, war and in addition, quite radically, by the Prohibition in the thirties. 24 estates survived; today there are again over 300. And these few estates only managed to survive partly because they were allowed to produce the communion wine for the churches.

The rise and rediscovery of the valley can be attributed to energetic promoters such as Robert Mondavi who, from 1966 onwards, set to work indiscriminately and thoroughly, using a marketing strategy more suitable for the selling of a Porsche. Or Peter Newton with the Sterling Vineyards of 1972, a perfect setting on a hill overlooking the valley, bringing the observer out in goose bumps. The estate stands on the dome of a hill and is hidden behind the setting of a white "Cycladic" monastery. The visitors are aware of this from the outset because it adores the wine labels, a clever corporate identity measure that the estate owners pinched from the French chateaux. Inside the visitors are allowed to experience all the stages of wine-making in a self-guided tour; this was the first "wine museum" in the world with an incredibly high number of visitors (see also pp. 128 ff).

Robert Mondavi equally perfectly carries through the motif of his estate, with a simple tower and an annexed reception building, to his letter-head and wine labels, and he combines his wine with lively vernissages and summer fairs in the shady courtyard and on the green lawn of his estate. "Die Zeit" acknowledged the creed of the Napa wine-growers: "Wine and culture belong together, wine is not like whisky, wine is not an alcoholic drink. Wine is art. Wine is life!"[5]

From the Wine-Growing Farm to the Wine Factory

Only those who look carefully will notice the rather large wine factory to the side of the Mondavi Winery, hidden behind high walls and greenery. The Napa Valley does not simply house intimate wine-growing farms. In addition to the fermentation cellar, tank farm, cellar and storeroom is a showroom, tasting room, shop, VIP and barbecue area – sometimes even a music room and wine library; together they form one of the most complex construction tasks in the world since the Americans approach wine-making like industrial barons, using tough marketing techniques, whilst in Europe there is still more of a demand for skilled craftsmanship (see also pp. 116 ff).

Sterling and Mondavi surprised everyone because up until that point estates resembled either "Hadrian's Villa or the Ponderosa"[6] (Raymond Ryan, architectural critic). With often unclear stylistic intentions the European examples were used as "scenic" architecture; alternatively, allegiance was shown, quite simply, to one's origins.

Thus it was these new Californian examples, above all the thoroughly aggressive marketing, which in the eighties woke the wine-growers in France from their slumber. Jean Dethier, who had since travelled around the Napa Valley, assumed the role of the prince performing the wakening kiss. The time was also ripe for new concepts. In the meantime the cultural landscape of Bordeaux was threatened. The landscape had been spoilt by development; faceless new buildings and extensions obstructed the view of old chateaux. The region was in danger of losing its identity if great wines were no longer to mature at the chateaux, but rather in a setting of commonplace architecture.

Competitions Alter Ways of Thinking and the Landscape
Several events occurred in the second half of the eighties in France that led to wine-growers in Bordeaux actually learning from the Napa Valley, thus allowing the trend to be broken. This could be attributed above all to the initial spark caused by the exhibition at the Centre Pompidou as six international architectural groups (Jeremy and Fenella Dixon with Mark Pimlott; Florence Lipsky, Pascal Rollet and Vincent Defos du Rau; Fernando Montes; Bertrand Nivelle;

Bruno Reichlin; Charles Vanderhove) were able to introduce their new "ideal type" of chateau. The designs for an imaginary location were reminiscent of knights' castles, river boats or a piece of revolutionary architecture from 1789. Sometimes design and decor bordered on over-the-top Disneyland architecture; they are clear-cut proof, however, that it is possible to use one's fantasy when tackling the task of constructing a chateau.

Another competition was, however, realised and was also presented at the time at the Centre Pompidou. In the wine-growing region of Durhart-Millon the Château Pichon-Longueville, a clearly structured chateau as could be found in the Loire, was missing a storage cellar and fermentation facilities. In August 1988 the two Parisian architects, Patrick Dillon and Jean de Gastines, won the competition (against the two Spaniards, Alberto Ustarroz and Manuel Iniguez, and the Parisian Fernando Montes). Even the competition program itself (see also pp. 68 ff) advertised a new dimension for a Bordeaux chateau: meanwhile growing tourism was demanding its dues and it was for this reason that the chateau, "chai" and "cuvier" found themselves up against competition: a sales pavilion, small museum, parking spaces and a "wine theatre". A lesson was learned: Jean Michel Cazes, the owner of Pichon-Longueville and in the meantime one of the important promoters of the new wine-architecture culture in Bordeaux, said at the time: "I want a classical wine chateau for the third millennium!". He got what he wished for: axial and symmetrical with obelisks, arches and volutes. A spectacle, albeit a concrete one, but which after only 10 years of wine-making and through worthy ageing was granted the status of "having always belonged".

Branding and Corporate Architecture

Two other chateaux likewise forcefully prepared the way for a new departure. For the reconstruction of the Château d'Arsac, an estate near Margeaux, Philippe and Francoise Raoux chose, in the midst of all the established estates, a strategy based on the sales-promoting effect of conspicuous architecture, or rather a strong blue colour, to be more precise (see also pp. 94 ff).

In the twenties Baron Philippe Rothschild had already left a memorial to himself in the form of his own wine-growing museum on his Mouton estate and had already hired Charles Sicilis, a theatre architect from Paris, to decorate it. In the eighties his cousin, Eric de Rothschild, had a new chai built for the post-modern play-actor, Richardo Bofill, on the neighbouring Lafite estate, the chai being "the particularly symbolic part of a chateau – the most treasured area"[7] (Jean Dethier). Because of its inner circular ring of columns it was felt to be very theatrical by many visitors; Baron de Rothschild, on the other hand, sees in it "a mysticism, which is as it were the spatial expression of our ethical image of wine"[8].

The baron also realised, however, that a "circular formation and thereby centrally organised arrangement has the advantage of cutting down on labour". Because the wine has to be transferred four times a year, at a rough estimate 300 kilometres less have to be travelled!

The message behind this statement is simple: it is not only a question of theatrics, symbolism and beauty; functionalism and efficacy are always important. Also important is the optimum conversion of the new, old type of "chateau" building, the wine-growing farm, which in the meantime has matured into a wine factory with a public marketing area. It is not merely style and aesthetics that are important.

A New Architecture of Wine

Meanwhile an opulent open-air museum of architecture was set up in the Napa Valley, allowing an amusing study of the different styles and fashions of the past 30 to 40 years, leading to the conclusion that with the level of quality reached here style really is only a matter of taste. Somehow most of the estates are convincing due to a likeable sophistication and a central concept (see also the portraits of the wine estates). The honour of having built the most meaningful, and also varied, prototypes of a new era undoubtedly belongs to the Americans in the Napa Valley. One reason for this may be that a large amount of fresh capital flows into the West. Suddenly investing in wine is considered refined. A second reason could be that architectonic visions are not hindered by clichés and age-old traditions. Everything is possible. Thirdly, the hedonistic days of the eighties were a hothouse for new ideas.

Napa's style is called "the best pluralism"! Here the "post-modern" Clos Pegase stands next to the Dominus Estate by the purists Herzog and de Meuron. In addition, there are the modernisations and reconstructions of buildings from the last century (Beringer, Coppola, Far Niente). But what Jean Dethier had feared never came true, namely that "the worst is to be found alongside the best"[9]. The influence of the "crazy people" such as Walt Disney's widow, the director Francis Ford Coppola and Bob Sinkskey who organised sought-after dinner parties in his wine catacombs, ensured quality and a veritable "breaking up" mood.

The most important communication, however, for architectonic development is how the countryside can be built on, now and in the future, and how a new understanding of a symbiosis of nature and culture could be created. Our resources have to be protected, even in less densely populated North California. In addition, large architectural dimensions have to be integrated: commercial and cultural buildings as well as show and work areas. If possible, the buildings are hidden in the landscape: for example in the form of a tunnel beneath the ground, which is good for the wine and has since led to tunnel construction companies in California becoming the most lucrative in the world.

Topography and grass also help when designing a facade. A prominent example is that of the American dependency of the royal Spanish purveyor to the court, Artesa, which has been dug from above into a pyramid-shaped hill. Finally, the buildings of Opus One land like UFOs on a grassy dome. Here in the Napa Valley the boundary between architecture, landscaping and type of land is blurred.

And one more thing is noticeable: the effect produced by Opus One is that of a synthesis of European and American building culture when a solid rock construction is coupled with an American roof veranda made of gleaming silver wood. What could be a more suitable purpose for building, in this case, than architecture for wine in which the art of living, climate, culture, architecture and wine intermingle – Napa as a global vineyard!

In the Médoc things have not been taken to such extremes. Maybe it's not considered at all necessary. After all, the wine prices here easily bring in repeatedly higher profits. The estates here are (as yet) not a tourist event as in the Napa Valley where the region's own railway train trudges though the valley and where the estates reserve special areas for barbecuing. In France the estate owners do not keep an open house, rather everything runs by discrete appointment.

The result is that the architects restrained themselves as far as exteriors were concerned and became guardians of tradition. Explosive, spatial wonders can be seen on the inside. An exclusive example is Ricardo Bofill's wine-cellar rotunda for Rothschild-Lafite. On the outside this estate is still, as before, a pleasant image of a French country idyll.

Even the architectonic show project Pichon-Longueville avoids leaning too heavily on 20th century architecture. The Chateaux Léoville-Poyferré and Branaire also prefer it this way and are turning into examples of a continued cautious approach to further building. The new building of the Domaines Henry Martin respects the trivial encumbrances of a village street. No, none of the examples from the Médoc really want to continue writing architectural history.

The French would rather do this in California itself. As is the case with "Dominus" in Yountville, in which French prominent figures such as Christian Mouiex, director of the famous Petrus Chateau in Pomerol, have shares. He could undoubtedly have made architectural his-tory here together with the Swiss avant-garde architects, Herzog and de Meuron. Dominus is everything: the past, present and future. A stone wall becomes the shell of an "archaic container" in which all the important aspects of a winery are housed. Dominus does not betray the roots of viniculture, coming, so

to speak, down to earth. On the inside it is modern, like a laboratory, full of surprises and adventures – a big success in fact.

The success of this building has enabled the "reductionists" and sensitive perceptive artists, Herzog and de Meuron, to add their names to the list of the best-ever architects of the 20th century; they have created a new chateau prototype. We are intrigued to find out how things will continue in the next millennium.

1 Robert Coustet: "Geschichte der Architektur im Weinbau" in: "Chateaux Bordeaux", Bern 1989, p. 63
2 Chateaux Bordeaux – Baukunst und Weinbau, The German Museum of Architecture, Bern 1989
3 John Doerper: Wine Country, California's Napa & Sonoma Valleys, pp. 12ff, Oakland, 1998
4 Sibylle Zehle: Herzblut und roter Wein in "Die Zeit" No. 6/99
5 ibid.
6 Raymond Ryan in Baumeister 7/98, pp. 36ff
7 Chateaux Bordeaux, p. 173
8 ibid.
9 ibid. p. 180

L'architecture du vin
Remarques sur le renouveau d'une
ancienne typologie de construction

Dirk Meyhöfer

Aussi merveilleusement archaïque et chargé d'histoire que soit le thème du vin, aussi nouvelle et surprenante – et au premier abord presque exotique – peut sembler la volonté de voir dans l'architecture du vin un thème d'avant-garde. Des domaines viticoles, à l'origine le plus souvent des fermes viticoles, il en existe depuis déjà plus de 2 000 ans. Comme il s'agit pour l'essentiel de variations autour d'un ensemble composé d'un manoir – le "Château" –, d'une ferme et de dépendances, il ne peut pas exister de discussion architecturale à propos d'une typologie de construction, comme on peut en mener sur les cathédrales, les gares ou les banques. On a pourtant déjà très bien pu écrire une "Histoire de l'architecture viticole", dans laquelle on trouve la phrase suivante: "L'architecture dans les vignobles (de Bordeaux) doit prendre en considération l'ensemble des composants d'un domaine et on ne peut rien laisser au hasard"[1]. Nous y reviendrons, mais il vaut mieux commencer par la fin et cet événement qui a mené, sinon à la découverte, au moins à la redécouverte de ce thème: la grande exposition "Châteaux Bordeaux" organisée en 1988 par le Centre Pompidou, un lieu d'avant-garde renommé, dédié à l'architecture et au design. Ce fut la percée!

Jean Dethier, un architecte et créateur d'exposition belge résidant à Paris, connu pour son flair pour les thèmes d'architecture en vogue, devait écrire dans les années 80 une page d'architecture dans les colonnes du plus grand magazine viticole bordelais: "L'Amateur de Bordeaux". Il a reconnu très vite, que: "L'art le plus important que la société des propriétaires viticoles a décidé d'encourager avec une exceptionnelle unanimité, c'est l'architecture"[2].

Dans la pratique, cela veut dire que le vigneron du Bordelais a déjà réussi au début du 19ème siècle à faire d'un nom à la sonorité aristocratique – le Château – une image de marque qui impose une association inconsciente reliant le vin à une somptueuse architecture. Même si dans le monde entier les consommateurs sont persuadés du contraire, la dénomination "Château" ne veut pas dire grand chose sur la qualité architecturale de la ferme viticole (ce n'est souvent pas plus que ça!) – où le vin est produit. Il y a actuellement plusiers milliers de Châteaux dans le Bordelais. Certains parmi eux, comme le fier Château Margaux, semblent habités par une âme antique, mais d'autres, au mode de construction schématique et banal, ne possèdent même pas le charme d'une ferme moyenne. Tous pourtant profitent de la légende dans laquelle Jean Dethier voit l'exemple précoce et parfait d'une identité corporative symbolisée par l'architecture.

Un domaine viticole, qu'est ce que c'est?

Dans les siècles passés, le domaine viticole était en général composé de quatre parties formant un tout: le Château, le chai, le cuvier et le vignoble. Dans le cuvier sont rangées les grandes cuves – aujourd'hui en général des cylindres en acier inoxydable – dans lesquelles le vin fermente. Dans le chai reposent les barriques, des tonneaux faits à la main d'une contenance d'environ 225 litres, où le vin, après le processus de fermentation, mûrit au moins deux ans avant d'être mis en bouteilles (voir l'article de Peter C. Hubschmid: "L'art du vigneron", pages 220 et suivantes).

Il est indiscutable que la production de vin dans le Bordelais remonte à l'époque romaine. Mais c'est seulement à la fin du 17ème siècle, c'est-à-dire très tard par rapport à d'autres vignobles, que l'on a commencé à utiliser pour la culture de la vigne le sol alluvionnaire et le climat océanique chaud, humide et salé des régions de la Gironde et de la Garonne. Les grands domaines de l'embouchure de la Gironde ont connu leur première éclosion entre 1840 et 1870, juste au moment où fleurissait en architecture un mélange de styles exubérant. Ce n'est donc pas une surprise si la traversée du Médoc devient une promenade aventureuse à travers l'histoire de l'architecture: l'Egypte, la Grèce, le Gothique, Palladio, la Renaissance, le Baroque et – très souvent – le Classicisme. Qui compte les modèles? Qui recherche les associations éclectiques? On a parfois l'impression d'avoir dans un seul Château le témoignage de la variété des styles de l'Orient et de l'Occident.

Illustration de cette démonstration, le Château Cos d'Estournel (voir aussi pages 38 et suivantes), construit en 1830, ressemble à un mirage. Au nord de Pauillac et du

domaine Lafite-Rothschild, ses halls décorés de petites tours graciles, qui apparaissent soudain dans un virage au-dessus des verts vignobles, sont chargés d'une fantaisie si orientale qu'un éléphant ou un chameau pourraient surgir à chaque instant sans paraître incongrus. Ces deux domaines (Lafite-Rothschild et Cos d'Estournel) ont d'ailleurs survécu bravement à une série d'épreuves qui a duré près d'un siècle et qui n'est terminée que depuis une trentaine d'années. Pendant cette phase, le phylloxéra, le mildiou, les crises économiques et les guerres qui se sont succédées ont mis en péril l'existence des vignerons du Bordelais. On a du mal à imaginer cette précarité à une époque où les grands crus cotés en bourse sont presque devenus une valeur de placement.

Ce n'est que depuis les années 60 – avec une petite pause pendant la crise pétrolière – que l'on remonte la pente rapidement et que l'on a tendance à faire des investissements d'envergure. C'est donc seulement depuis peu qu'il est possible de poursuivre la grande tradition architecturale du 19ème siècle.

Encore fallait-il un messager génial faisant la relation entre l'ancien et le nouveau monde, comme Jean Dethier, un provocateur riche et plein de vie. Dans ce cas pour ainsi dire le fils illégitime du père, qui entre temps – on peut livrer ce secret – a été adopté avec amour.

De Bordeaux à Napa valley

Au 19ème siècle, la Californie est entrée en lice, avec sa charmante Napa valley, située à une heure au nord de San Francisco. "Un véritable jardin d'Eden", comme l'écrit John Doeper, le rédacteur du journal gastronomique "Pacific Epicure"[3] dans une autodescription complaisante, "un patchwork coloré de Provence, de Toscane, de Bordeaux, de Champagne et de vallée du Rhin, avec du soleil comme à Mexico et le rude vent du Pacifique qui apporte la pluie; avec un climat, un ciel et un vin violents".

Jusque dans les années 60, le vin de Napa valley n'était pas pris au sérieux en France. Le baron Philippe de Rothschild le considérait alors comme un "breuvage industriel, trop épicé et non adapté au marché mondial"[4] et il n'était pas seul à exprimer cette opinion.

Napa valley avait derrière elle une histoire qui rappelait celle du Bordelais. C'est vers 1839 que des vignerons allemands ont commencé à planter en Californie de la vigne, essentiellement du gewurztraminer. Le phylloxéra, les guerres et surtout la prohibition radicale dans les années 30 ont pratiquement tout annihilé. Seuls 24 domaines viticoles ont survécu, certains uniquement grâce à l'autorisation de produire du vin de messe. Aujourd'hui, il y a à nouveau 300 domaines dans la vallée.

La redécouverte et l'ascension de Napa valley sont dus essentiellement à des promoteurs pleins d'énergie, comme Robert Mondavi qui, à partir de 1966, s'est mis à l'œuvre de manière très organisée, avec un marketing aussi agressif que s'il voulait vendre des Porsche. Peter Newton, lui, a réalisé en 1972 son Sterling Vineyards, parfaitement mis en scène

sur un promontoire, avec une vue sur la vallée qui donne la chair de poule. Situé au sommet d'une colline, son domaine se cache dans les coulisses d'un monastère blanc inspiré de ceux des Cyclades. Les visiteurs reconnaissent immédiatement cet ensemble bâti qui orne les étiquettes; une mesure habile, copiée sur celle des propriétaires viticoles français des "Châteaux", qui renforce l'image de marque du domaine. A l'intérieur, les visiteurs peuvent se promener librement en suivant un circuit qui leur permet de découvrir toutes les étapes de la fabrication du vin. C'est le premier Musée du vin du monde et il reçoit un nombre de visiteurs impressionnant (voir pages 128 et suivantes).

Robert Mondavi reproduit lui aussi sur ses étiquettes et sur son papier à lettres le motif de son domaine, composé d'une tour couverte de végétation et d'un bâtiment d'accueil jeté comme un pont. Il relie aussi l'image de son vin avec des vernissages très gais et des garden-parties à l'ombre de sa cour intérieure. "Die Zeit" a rendu hommage à ce vigneron de Napa valley en citant son credo: "Le vin et la culture sont liés. Le vin n'est pas comme le whisky, ce n'est pas une boisson alcoolisée. Le vin est un art. Le vin, c'est la vie!"[5]

De la ferme viticole à l'usine à vin
Seul celui qui regarde avec attention remarque, à côté de la tour de Mondavi Winery, l'usine à vin cachée derrière de hauts murs et des barrières végétales. A Napa valley, on ne rencontre pas de fermes viticoles intimes. A côté du pressoir, du chai, du cellier et des entrepôts, il y a toujours des salons de dégustations, des salles d'exposition, des boutiques, des aires de loisirs et des espaces pour les hôtes de marque, parfois même des salles de musique et des bibliothèques du vin. La combinaison de ces fonctions très variées compose un des programmes de construction les plus complexes du monde, car les américains abordent la production du vin comme des barons d'industrie. Ils jouent sur tous les registres du marketing, alors qu'en Europe c'est encore l'artisanat qui est le plus souvent demandé (voir pages 116 et suivantes).

Sterling et Mondavi ont surpris tout le monde. Jusque là, les domaines ressemblaient, selon l'expression du critique d'architecture Raymond Ryan, "à la Villa d'Hadrien ou à la Ponderosa"[6]. Avec une volonté stylistique pas toujours très sûre, on y reproduisait les modèles européens pour créer un décor d'architecture ou on avait tout simplement recours aux exemples locaux.

Ce sont les nouveaux modèles californiens, et en particulier leur marketing agressif, qui dans les années 80 ont réveillé les vignerons français de leur sommeil de "belle au bois dormant". Jean Dethier, qui entre temps avait fait le voyage à Napa valley, a pris le rôle du prince charmant. Le moment était venu pour développer de nouveaux concepts. Le paysage culturel du Bordelais était en danger. La campagne était soumise au mitage, des bâtiments nouveaux et des extensions gâchaient la vue sur les anciens Châteaux. On voyait pointer le risque d'une perte d'identité si les grands vins ne mûrissaient plus dans ces Châteaux, mais dans le décor d'une architecture internationale banalisée.

La concurrence, moteur de la transformation des modes de pensée et du paysage

Dans la deuxième moitié des années 80, plusieurs événements ont montré aux vignerons français qu'ils avaient quelque chose à apprendre de Napa valley. C'est essentiellement l'exposition du Centre Pompidou qui a servi de détonateur à la rupture de tendance. Six équipes d'architectes (Jeremy et Fenella Dixon avec Mark Pimlott; Florence Lipsky, Pascal Rollet et Vincent Defos du Rau; Fernando Montes; Bertrand Nivelle; Bruno Reichlin; Charles Vander-hove) ont pu y présenter leur modèle idéal du "nouveau Château". Les projets, situés sur un lieu imaginaire, rappelaient des châteaux forts, des bateaux de rivière ou l'architecture révolutionnaire de 1789. Conception et décor frisaient parfois une architecture exubérante à la Disney Land, mais ils prouvaient noir sur blanc que l'on peut attaquer la construction d'un Château avec fantaisie. C'était uniquement un concours d'idées.

Un autre concours, présenté lui aussi au Centre Pompidou, a été suivi de réalisation. Dans le domaine Duhart-Millon, il manquait au bâtiment existant – le Château Pichon-Longueville, une construction clairement composée et toute en hauteur, comme on en trouve sur les bords de la Loire – une cave et des installations pour la fermentation. En août 1988, les architectes parisiens Patrick Dillon et Jean de Gastines ont gagné le concours contre Fernando Montes, un autre parisien, et une équipe espagnole composée d'Alberto Ustarroz et Manuel Iniguez. Déjà le programme de ce concours (voir aussi pages 68 et suivantes) annonçait une nouvelle dimension pour la conception d'un Château bordelais. On avait compris que le développement du tourisme réclamait désormais son tribut: Château, chai et cuvier y étaient mis en concurrence avec un pavillon de vente, un petit musée, un "théâtre du vin" et un parking. Jean Michel

Cazes, le propriétaire de Pichon-Longueville – entre-temps un des principaux promoteurs de la nouvelle architecture du vin - disait à l'époque: "Je veux un château du vin classique pour le troisième millénaire". Il l'a obtenu: axé et symétrique avec des obélisques, des arcs et des volutes. Un spectacle – en béton, il est vrai - qui après seulement dix ans, recouvert de vigne vierge et porteur d'une vénérable patine, a déjà pris le statut de ce qui est là depuis toujours.

Architecture "Branding & corporate"

Deux autres domaines ont préparé eux aussi énergiquement le terrain pour un nouveau départ. Pour la reconstruction du Château d'Arsac, un domaine proche du Château Margaux situé au milieu de tous les domaines bien établis, Philippe et Françoise Raoux ont choisi une stratégie basée sur l'influence commerciale d'une architecture sortant de l'ordinaire. Dans la pratique, cela veut dire qu'ils ont créé un contraste et introduit du bleu vif en façade (voir pages 94 et suivantes).

Dans les années 20, le baron Philippe de Rothschild avait déjà posé une première pierre en créant son propre musée de la viticulture sur son domaine de Mouton. Pour la décoration, il avait alors fait appel à Charles Siclis, un architecte de théâtre parisien. Dans les années 80, son cousin Eric de Rothschild a choisi le "comédien" postmoderne Ricardo Bofill pour construire un nouveau chai sur le domaine voisin de Lafite. Le chai est selon Jean Dethier: "l'élément particulièrement symbolique d'un Château, le lieu le plus respecté"[7]. A cause du cercle de colonnes placé à l'intérieur,

beaucoup de visiteurs trouvent cet espace très théâtral. Le baron de Rothschild y voit lui: "une mystique qui représente d'une certaine manière l'expression spatiale de notre éthique du vin"[8].

Il fait aussi remarquer que "la composition circulaire avec une distribution centrale a apporté l'avantage d'une diminution de la main d'œuvre". Le vin doit être en effet changé de place quatre fois par an et cette disposition a apporté une économie annuelle d'environ 300 kilomètres sur le chemin parcouru par le personnel.

Le message qui se cache derrière cette déclaration est simple: il n'est pas seulement question ici de théâtre, de symbole et de beauté, mais aussi de fonctionnalité et d'efficacité. Pour obtenir la transformation optimale de l'ancien type de construction "Château" - la ferme viticole - en une "usine à vin" avec un espace marketing ouvert au public, on ne s'occupe pas seulement de style et d'esthétique.

Une nouvelle architecture du vin

Il existe maintenant à Napa valley un vaste musée de plein air de l'architecture. Il permet une étude amusante des modes des 30 ou 40 dernières années et amène à la conclusion que le style est vraiment une affaire de goût. Pourtant, à leur manière, la plupart des domaines ont un parti architectural affirmé et un aspect culturel sympathique qui arrivent à convaincre (voir aussi les descriptions des différents domaines). C'est sans aucun doute aux américains de Napa valley que revient l'honneur d'avoir réalisé les prototypes les plus variés, et aussi les plus convaincants, d'une nouvelle ère. Les raisons sont peut être liées aux capitaux frais qui coulent vers l'ouest: il est devenu soudain très chic d'investir dans le vin et aucun cliché, aucune tradition incrustée, n'y entrave les visions architecturales. En Californie, tout est possible et la période hédoniste des années 80 a agi comme une "serre à idée".

A Napa valley, style est synonyme de "meilleur pluralisme"! Ici, le Clos Pégase postmoderne voisine avec le Dominus Estate des puristes Herzog et de Meuron. S'y ajoutent la modernisation et la reconstruction de bâtiments du siècle dernier, comme dans les domaines Beringer, Coppola et Far Niente. Ce que Jean Dethier craignait, c'est-à-dire que "le pire côtoie le meilleur"[9] ne s'est heureusement pas produit. L'influence des "crazy people", comme la veuve de Walt Disney, le metteur en scène Francis Ford Coppola ou Bob

Sinskey, qui organise des dîners très prisés dans ses cata-combes à vin, a préservé la qualité et favorisé un véritable renouveau.

La question la plus importante pour le développement de l'architecture est la suivante: Comment, dans le présent et le futur, peut-on introduire une construction dans le paysage et créer une nouvelle prise de conscience de la symbiose entre nature et culture? Même en Californie du Nord, une région très peu peuplée, il faut protéger les ressources et intégrer dans le paysage des programmes de taille importan-te comprenant constructions pour la production, bâtiments culturels, espaces d'exposition et de vente. Lorsque c'est pos-sible, on peut dissimuler les réalisations, par exemple en souterrain, dans un tunnel, ce qui est d'ailleurs bénéfique pour le vin. Depuis que cette mesure s'est généralisée, la direction d'une entreprise de construction de tunnel n'est nulle part aussi lucrative qu'en Californie!

La topographie et une couverture végétalisée peuvent aussi apporter une aide à la conception des parois exté-rieures: la dépendance américaine du fournisseur de la cour royale espagnole, Artesa, est enterrée dans une pyramide; les bâtiments de Opus one sont posés comme un ovni sur le haut d'une colline engazonnée. A Napa valley, les frontières entre architecture, paysage et Land art ont été effacées.

On y trouve aussi la synthèse entre les cultures constructives européenne et américaine, comme à Opus One, lorsqu`un corps de bâtiment en lourdes pierres rencontre une véranda américaine en bois au gris argenté. Quel type de construc-tion serait mieux adapté à une architecture pour le vin, où se mêlent art de vivre, climat et culture. Napa valley, le vignoble global!

Dans le Médoc, on n'est pas allé aussi loin, sans doute parce qu'on n'en a pas besoin. Là, on ajoute régulièrement, et en toute légèreté, un zéro au prix du vin. Les Châteaux n'y sont (pas encore!) un événement touristique, contraire-ment à Napa valley où les domaines ont leur propre train qui se traîne dans la vallée et des zones de loisirs pour bar-becue. En France, les portes ne sont pas grandes ouvertes et il faut prendre avant la visite un rendez-vous discret.

Les architectes y ont en conséquence protégé la tradition et sont restés très réservés en ce qui concerne la conception des façades. A l'intérieur, par contre, on peut découvrir des espaces qui sont des miracles explosifs, comme la rotonde de Ricardo Bofill pour le chai de Lafite-Rothschild, domaine qui conserve à l'extérieur l'image charmante et idyllique d'un Château français.

Même le projet "architecturalement expérimental" de Pichon-Longueville à l'extérieur des avances trop visibles vers l'architecture du 20ème siècle. Les Châteaux Léoville-Poyferré et Branaire sont eux aussi deux exemples d'exten-sions pleines d'égards pour l'existant et le nouveau bâtiment des Domaines Henri Martin respecte les caractéristiques d'une rue de village banale. Non, vraiment, aucun des exemples du Médoc ne mérite d'être inscrit dans l'histoire de l'architecture.

Les projets exceptionnels, les français préfèrent les réaliser en Californie. Plusieurs personnalités françaises ont participé à la création de Dominus Estate à Yountville, comme Christian Moueix, le director du célèbre Château Petrus à Pomerol. Avec les architectes suisses d'avant-garde Herzog et de Meuron, il apporte là très certainement sa pierre à l'histoire de l'architecture. Dominus Estate, c'est tout: le passé, le présent et le futur. Un mur en pierre devient enveloppe d'un "container archaïque" dans lequel sont intégrées toutes les fonctions d'une ferme viticole. Dominus Estate ne trahit pas les racines de la fabrication du vin: il vient pour ainsi dire "directement de la terre". A l'intérieur, c'est moderne comme un laboratoire, plein de surprises et de découvertes. Une grande réussite, tout simplement.

Avec cette réalisation, les minimalistes et sensibles artistes de la perception que sont Herzog et de Meuron se sont inscrits sur la liste des "éternellement meilleurs architectes du 20ème siècle". Ils ont aussi créé un nouveau prototype de Château. Nous attendons avec impatience ce qui va se passer au siècle prochain.

1 Robert Coustet, Geschichte der Architektur im Weinbau, dans "Châteaux Bordeaux – Baukunst und Weinbau", édité par le Musée allemand de l'architecture, Berne 1989, page 63
2 "Châteaux Bordeaux – Baukunst und Weinbau", édité par le Musée allemand de l'architecture, Berne 1989
3 John Doeper, guide "Wine Country, California's Napa & Sonoma valleys", Oakland 1998, pages 12 et suivantes
4 Sibylle Zehle, "Herzblut und roter Wein", dans "Die Zeit", n° 6/1999

5 ibid
6 Raymond Ryan dans "Baumeister", n° 7/1998, pages 36 et suivantes
7 "Châteaux Bordeaux – Baukunst und Weinbau", édité par le Musée allemand de l'architecture, Berne 1989, page 173
8 ibid
9 ibid, page 180

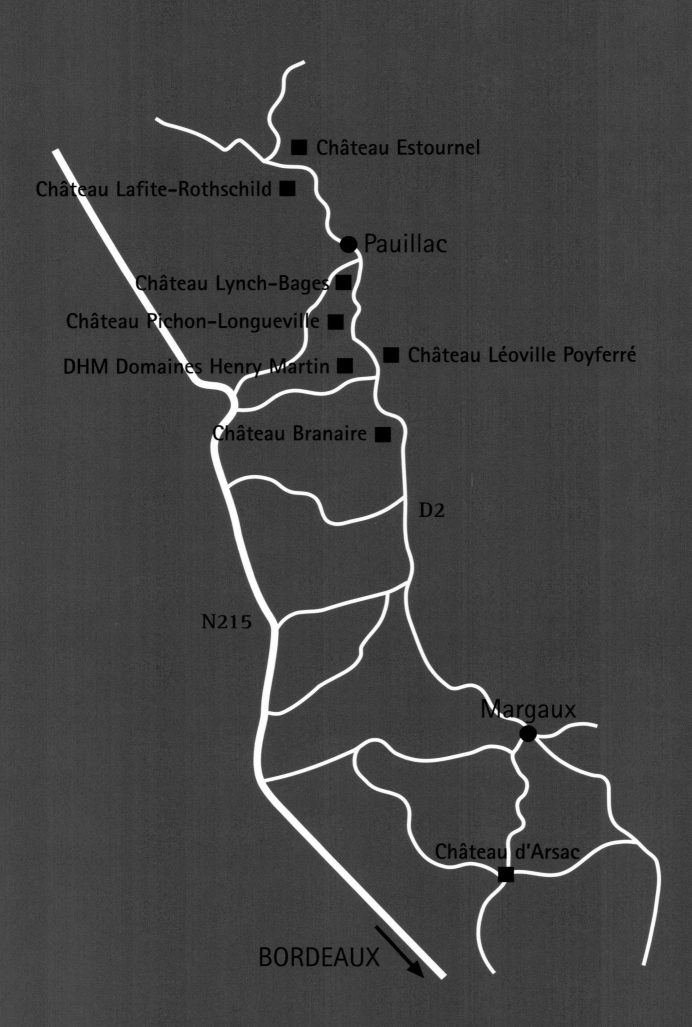

Château Estournel

Château Lafite-Rothschild

Pauillac

Château Lynch-Bages

Château Pichon-Longueville

Château Léoville Poyferré

DHM Domaines Henry Martin

Château Branaire

D2

N215

Margaux

Château d'Arsac

BORDEAUX

Bordeaux

Die von uns ausgesuchten Weingüter im Bordelais liegen überwiegend im Médoc, jener sanft hügeligen grünen Landschaft zwischen Atlantik und Gironde, die mit guten Böden und auffrischenden Winden gesegnet ist. Das flache Land an Atlantik und Gironde unterwirft sich der unendlichen Schraffur der Rebstöcke, die dem Landstrich Weltruhm gebracht haben und beim Connaisseur Sehnsüchte wecken. Unterbrochen werden die Weingärten allein durch anschmiegsame Mauern, eherne Kruzifixe, bullige Türme. Und natürlich durch die weltberühmten Châteaux. Die Anreise erfolgt am besten über die Stadt Bordeaux am linken Ufer der Garonne auf der N215 oder D2 in Richtung Margaux/Pauillac. Die alte Flußhafenstadt Bordeaux, kultureller Mittelpunkt der Region, hat in den letzten Jahren den Strukturwandel zur Dienstleistungsstadt geschafft, ohne seine idyllische südländische Atmosphäre aufzugeben.

The estates we have selected in the Bordeaux region are situated mainly in the Médoc, that green landscape with its gently rolling hills lying between the Atlantic and Gironde, which is blessed with good soils and fresh winds. The flat land of the Atlantic and Gironde has given itself up to the endless rows of vines, which have brought international fame to the area, awakening yearnings in connoisseurs. The vineyards are interrupted only by smooth walls, iron crucifixes, and chunky towers. And, naturally, also by the world-famous chateaux. The journey is best conducted via the city of Bordeaux along the left bank of the Garonne onto the N215 or D2 in the direction of Margaux/Pauillac. In the past few years the old river-port town and cultural centre has managed to undergo a structural change into a service town, without giving up its idyllic southern European atmosphere.

Les domaines du Bordelais que nous avons choisis se trouvent presque tous dans le Médoc, un paysage aux douces collines vertes, situé entre l'Atlantique et la Gironde et béni par son sol et ses vents rafraîchissants. La plaine qui borde la Gironde est couverte de rangées de vignes interminables qui ont apporté à cette bande de terre une réputation internationale et éveillé le désir des connaisseurs. Les vignobles ne sont interrompus que par des murets en pierre, des crucifix d'antan, des tours massives et naturellement les Châteaux mondialement célèbres. On y accède de préférence à partir de Bordeaux, le long de la rive gauche de la Garonne, sur la nationale 215 ou la départementale 2 en direction de Margaux et de Pauillac. La vieille cité portuaire, centre culturel de la région, a réussi au cours des dernières années sa mutation structurelle en une ville de services, sans perdre pour autant son atmosphère méridionale idyllique.

Château
Cos d'Estournel

Ex Oriente | Ein Reisender im Jahre 1838 stellt beim Anblick von „Cos d'Estournel" fest: „Eigentlich kann man dieses Château keinem Stil zuschreiben; es ist weder griechisch noch gotisch, sondern recht heiter und eher nach der chinesischen Art." Das hat der französische Romancier Stendhal richtig erkannt: das Weingut wollte so orientalisch sein wie seine wichtigsten Kunden, die aus dem Fernosten stammten. Denn es war eine Art Verkaufshilfe oder, wie man heute sagen würde, Marketing, wenn die maurischen Bögen und chinesischen Pagodendächer der exotischen Klientel Heimat vorgaukeln sollten.

Ex Orient | In the year 1838 a traveller remarked at the sight of "Cos d'estournel" that "it is actually impossible to ascribe a particular style to this chateau; it is neither Greek nor Gothic, but has a rather serene, Chinese-like style." The French novelist, Stendhal, was right in his observation: the estate wished to be as oriental as its most important clients who came from the Far East. The Moorish arches and Chinese pagoda roofs were representative of the exotic clientele's homeland and were thus used as a kind of selling aid, or marketing ploy as it would be called today.

L'influence de l'Orient | En 1838, un voyageur a constaté en regardant le Cos d'Estournel: "En fait, on ne peut relier ce château à aucun style; il n'est ni grec, ni gothique, mais très cocasse et plutôt influencé par l'art chinois". Le romancier français Stendhal l'a reconnu avec justesse: le domaine voulait être aussi oriental que ses meilleurs clients qui venaient d'Extrême-Orient. C'était autant une manière de favoriser la vente - ou comme on le dirait maintenant, de faire du marketing - que d'amuser la clientèle exotique en imitant les arcs mauresques et les toits relevés des pagodes chinoises.

[1]

Der ursprüngliche Besitzer Louis Gaspard
d'Estournel ist über soviel Architekturbegei-
sterung verarmt verstorben, sein Weinschloß
auf den Hügeln in Saint-Estèphe oberhalb
von Pauillac ist allerdings seit 1990 Stück
für Stück rekonstruiert und behutsam erweitert worden. Was von der Straße aus gesehen, dreihüftig die Vision eines orientali-
schen Versailles erzeugt, verbirgt hinter den
in der Abendsonne wundersam leuchtenden
Sandsteinwänden Cuvier und Chai. Genau in
der Mitte der Fassade schiebt sich immer
wieder die geschnitzte Haupttür, die zum
Weinkeller führt, ins Auge: Sie stammt von
einem Sultanspalast aus Sansibar.

The original owner, Louis Gaspard d'Estournel, died as poor man over so much architectural enthusiasm; since 1990, however, his
wine chateau in the hills of Saint-Estèphe
above Paulliac has been reconstructed piece
by piece and discreetly extended. That which,
seen from the road, creates a three-towered
vision of an oriental Versailles, conceals the
cuvier and chai behind its sandstone walls
glowing wonderously in the evening sun.
Exactly in the middle of the facade the carv-
ed main door, leading to the wine cellar,
repeatedly catches one's eye: it originates
from a sultan's palace in Sansibar.

A cause de son enthousiasme débordant, le
propriétaire d'origine, Louis Gaspard d'Estournel, est mort dans l'indigence. Son château,
posé sur une colline à Saint-Estèphe, au-dessus de Pauillac, est cependant reconstruit
morceau par morceau depuis 1990 et a été
agrandi avec beaucoup de respect. Ce que l'on
peut voir de la route, et qui offre la vision
d'un Versailles oriental, cache cuvier et chai
derrière des murs en calcaire, miroitant admi-
rablement au soleil couchant. Placée exacte-
ment au centre de la façade, la porte sculptée
qui mène au chai saute aux yeux des visiteurs:
c'est une réplique de celle du palais du sultan
de Zanzibar.

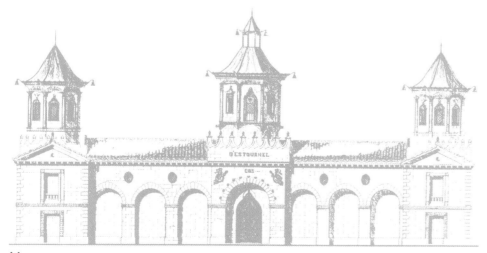

[2]

[1] Exotisch: Eine
Palmenallee führt ins
Innere des Château
[2] Ansichtszeichnung
der Hauptfront
[3] Aus Sansibar: Detail
des Hauptportals

[1] Exotic: an avenue
lined with palms leads
to the interior of the
chateau
[2] Drawing of the view
of the main facade
[3] From Sansibar: detail
of the main portal

[1] Exotique: une allée de
palmiers conduit au cœur
du Château.
[2] Dessin de la façade
principale
[3] Souvenir de Zanzibar:
détail du portail d'entrée

[1]

Wem es erlaubt ist, hinauf zu den arabesken Glockentürmen zu steigen, blickt nach hinten auf eine bewegte Dachlandschaft aus uralten roten Ziegeln. Wer unten bleibt, erlebt unter einer riesigen Korkeiche und im luftigen Atlantikwind ein bißchen von dem, was diese Landschaft hier geprägt hat.

Umso stärker ist der Kontrast, wenn man seitlich des Hauptgebäudes in die Hofanlage eindringt: Eine mit Palmen bestandene Allee führt zu einem kleinen Museum, wo die Geschichte dieses Weinguts mit vielen schönen Exponaten eindringlich erzählt wird, und dem pastellfarbem Probierraum. Ob innen, wo im Chai orientalisches Schnitzwerk die Weinfässer flankiert, oder außen: Stendhal hatte recht, das Wort vom Château hat hier eine neue Dimension gefunden. Und das schon zu Beginn des 19. Jahrhunderts.

Anyone being allowed to climb up to the arabesque bell towers looks back onto a colourful landscape of roofs made of ancient red tiles. Whoever stays below, standing beneath a massive cork-oak in the breezy Atlantic wind, experiences a little of the character of the landscape here.

The contrast is even greater upon finding one's way into the courtyard area at the side of the main building: an avenue lined with palms leads to a small museum, where the history of this estate is impressively told with the aid of many beautiful exhibits, and to a pastel-coloured, tiled tasting room. Whether within, where wood carvings flank the wine barrels in the chai, or without, Stendhal was right: the word "chateau" had found a new dimension here, as early as the beginning of the 19th Century.

Le privilégié autorisé à monter en haut des clochetons peut admirer un paysage de toits en antiques tuiles rouges. Celui qui reste en bas découvre, sous les énormes chênes-lièges et dans le vent vif de l'Atlantique, un peu de ce qui a donné son empreinte à ce paysage.

Le contraste est particulièrement fort lorsqu'on pénètre dans la cour par le côté du bâtiment principal. Une allée plantée de palmiers mène à un petit musée où l'histoire du domaine est racontée de ma-nière émouvante avec beaucoup de beaux objets, et à un salon de dégustation, couvert de carrelages aux tons pastels. Dans le chai, les tonneaux sont flanqués de sculptures sur bois d'inspiration orientale. Stendhal avait raison: à l'extérieur comme à l'intérieur, le mot "Château" a trouvé ici – déjà au début du 19ème siècle – une nouvelle dimension.

[2]

[3]

[4]

[1] Hofansicht mit historischem Wasserturm
[2] Im Chai: orientalisches Detail zwischen europäischen Eichenfässern
[3] Degustation: Preisgekrönte Weine warten auf Käufer
[4] Perspektivische Zeichnung der Gesamtanlage

[1] View of the courtyard with its historic water tower
[2] In the chai: oriental detail between European oak barrels
[3] Tasting: prize-winning wines wait for buyers
[4] Drawing of the entire estate in perspective

[1] La cour avec le château d'eau historique
[2] Dans le chai: détail oriental entre des tonneaux en chêne européens
[3] Dégustation: des vins primés attendent les acheteurs
[4] Perspective de l'ensemble des installations

Château
Lafite–Rothschild

Theatralischer Ort der Vernunft | Ein Weg zu Ricardo Bofills unterirdischem Werk führt durch einen hunderte Meter langen Kellergang. Geschätzte 80.000 Flaschen Cru Bordeaux, die „Familienreserve" liegen in den seitlichen Katakomben, die ältesten Flaschen stammen aus dem Jahrgang 1797 (Siebzehnhundertsiebenundneunzig!). Der schmale Gang, der durch flackernde Kerzen gerade so erhellt wird, daß man sein kafkaeskes Ende ahnen kann, macht deutlich: hier wird inszeniert! Am Gang-Ende liegt eine kleine Rotunde, dann folgt ein gewaltiges Achteck: der Chai. Den katalanischen Architekten Ricardo Bofill kennt man als Meister der großen Geste, leider stecken hinter - seinen gewaltigen Säulenfassaden dann oft harmlose Sozialwohnungsgrundrisse, die alles zu einer potemkinschen Posse verkommen lassen. Hier auf „Lafite" stimmt auch die dritte Dimension.

Theatrical place of reason | A path to Ricardo Bofill's underground work leads through a one-hundred-metre long cellar passageway. An estimated 80 000 bottles of Cru Bordeaux, the "family reserves" lie in the catacombs to the side, the oldest bottles dating back to the year 1797 (seventeen hundred and ninety-seven!). The narrow corridor, illuminated by flickering candles just enough to give the merest suspicion of its Kafkaesque end, clarifies the picture: here, everything is stage-managed! At the end of the corridor is a small rotunda, behind which is an immense octagon: the chai. The Catalan architect, Ricardo Bofill, is known as the master of great gestures; unfortunately, harmless council flat plans are often concealed behind his massive columned facades, which reduce everything to a farcical sham. Here at "Lafite" the third dimension is also right.

Théâtre et raison | Le chemin vers l'œuvre souterraine de Ricardo Bofill se fait à travers un couloir de 100 mètres de long. Environ 80 000 bouteilles de "Cru Bordeaux" – la réserve de la famille – reposent dans des caves latérales. Les plus anciennes datent de 1797 (mille sept cent quatre-vingt dix-sept!). L'étroit couloir, éclairé seulement par des chandeliers afin que l'on puisse imaginer une fin kafkaïenne, l'exprime clairement: ici, on met en scène! Au bout du couloir se trouve une rotonde, puis un immense octogone: le chai. On sait que l'architecte catalan Ricardo Bofill est le maître du "grand geste". Malheureusement, il n'y a souvent derrière ses immenses façades à colonnades que des plan banals de logements sociaux qui transforment l'ensemble en bouffonnerie. Ici, à Lafite, la troisième dimension est en accord avec le reste.

[1]

Kreisförmig umschließen die Fässer einen runden Säulenkranz im Zentrum des Kellers: Eine Bühne, eine Kathedrale oder ein Mausoleum für den Wein – die Begriffe verwischen sich, je nach Gemüt und Wahrnehmungslage des Betrachters. Es bleibt allen gemeinsam die große theatralische Geste, mit einer Orgie aus Raum und Licht. Der Eigentümer, Baron Eric de Rothschild, vergißt allerdings nie zu betonen, daß diese grandiose Form sehr wohl der Funktion folgt, weil sich genau nachweisen läßt, daß in einem zentral orientierten Keller insgesamt kürzere Wege für alle weinpflegerischen Arbeiten mit den Fässern zurückzulegen sind, als in einem länglichen Rechteck.

The barrels circle a rounded, columned area in the centre of the cellar: a stage, cathedral or mausoleum for the wine – the terms become blurred according to the observer's disposition and state of awareness. The one remaining common factor are the theatrical gestures, with an orgy of space and light. The owner, Baron Eric de Rothschild, never forgets to emphasise, however, that this grandiose form does indeed serve its function; it can be precisely proven that in a centrally orientated cellar, as opposed to an elongated rectangle, shorter ways have to be covered to carry out all the work involved in caring for the barrelled wine.

Placés en cercle, les tonneaux entourent une couronne de poteaux ronds disposés au centre du chai. Scène, cathédrale ou mausolée dédié au vin? Les définitions sont subjectives, selon l'état d'esprit de l'observateur ou sa sensibilité. Cela reste cependant un grand geste théâtral, avec une orgie d'espace et de lumière. Le propriétaire, le baron Eric de Rothschild, n'oublie cependant jamais de faire remarquer – et on peut le vérifier avec exactitude – que le chemin à parcourir pour les soins apportés au vin en tonneau est beaucoup plus court dans une cave circulaire que dans une cave rectangulaire.

Vorherige Seiten:
Details aus dem historischen Keller
[1] Gewollte Theatralik: kreisrunder Säulenkranz im neuen Chai (Ricardo Bofill, vgl. a. Titelbild)
[2] Geheimnisvoll: Zugang zum neuen Keller

Previous pages:
details from the historical cellar
[1] Artificial theatrics: circle of columns in the new chai (Ricardo Bofill, see also cover picture)
[2] Mysterious: entrance to the new cellar

Pages précédentes :
détails de la cave historique
[1] Volonté de théâtralité: le cercle de colonnes de Ricardo Bofill pour le nouveau chai
[2] Chargé de mystère: l'accès à la nouvelle cave

[1]

Und natürlich gilt die unterirdische Lage klimatisch als ideal und macht jede künstliche Klimatisierung überflüssig. Selbstverständlich besitzt das Kellerachteck einen direkten Ausgang nach draußen; besser sollte man es ein Portal mit fast ägyptischer Anmutung nennen, obwohl es streng genommen nur einen aus Beton gegossenen Einschnitt in den Weinberg darstellt. Bofill hatte ursprünglich eine schräggestellte Mauer mit zwei monumentalen Treppen an den Flanken vorgesehen. Die Vernunft des adligen Winzers, der zu recht eine Temperaturverschiebung im Keller an dieser Südseite zum Nachteil des Weines befürchtete, führte zur architektonisch „leiseren" Lösung. Auch sonst geben sich die Kellergebäude überirdisch ländlich, sittlich und konventionell: Nicht auffallen, heißt hier die passende Devise.

And, of course, the underground climate is classed as ideal, rendering any artificial air-conditioning superfluous. Naturally, the octagonal cellar has a direct exit to the outside; this would be better described as a portal with an Egyptian appearance, although strictly speaking it only constitutes a cleft in the vineyard, cast from concrete. Bofill had originally planned an obliquely positioned wall flanked by two monumental stairways. The good sense of the wine maker, who rightly feared that a temperature change in the cellar on this south side would be disadvantageous to the wine, led to a more "gentle" architectonic solution. Otherwise, the cellar buildings above ground also have a rural, moral and conventional appearance: remaining inconspicuous is the suitable motto in this case.

Naturellement, la situation souterraine offre un climat que l'on dit idéal et qui rend une ventilation mécanique superflue. Bien sûr, la cave octogonale possède un accès direct vers l'extérieur. Cela voudrait être un portail avec des références égyptiennes. Un observateur rigoureux n'y voit qu'une tranchée au milieu des vignes dans laquelle on a coulé du béton. Bofill avait prévu à l'origine un mur disposé en biais, flanqué de deux escaliers monumentaux. Le bon sens de l'aristocrate vigneron, qui avait raison de craindre, côté sud, une différence de température pouvant nuire à la qualité du vin, a conduit à une solution architecturale moins "bruyante". D'ailleurs, le reste des installations des caves souterraines est plutôt provincial, sage et conventionnel. Ici, la devise adoptée est: Ne pas se faire remarquer!

[2]

[3]

[1] Fast wie im alten
Ägypten: das mächtige
Portal des neuen Kellers
(Ricardo Bofill)
[2-3] Ländlich, sittlich:
Regionale Bautraditio-
nen bestimmen die Ar-
chitektur der übrigen
Kellergebäude auf Lafite-
Rothschild

[1] Almost like in ancient
Egypt: portal of the new
cellar (Ricardo Bofill)
[2-3] Rural, moral:
regional building tradi-
tions define the architecture of the other cellars
on the Lafite-Rothschild
estate

[1] Presque comme dans
l'ancienne Egypte: le
portail de Ricardo Bofill
pour la nouvelle cave
[2-3] Campagnard et
conformiste : les tradi-
tions de construction
régionales déterminent
l'architecture des autres
bâtiments du domaine
Lafite-Rothschild

Château
Pichon-Longueville

Der ewige Klassiker | Es herrschte sicher eine der aufgeregteren Phasen innerhalb der modernen Architektur, als 1988 der Wettbewerb für das Château Pichon-Longueville entschieden wurde. Das war kein gewöhnliches Bauwerk, sondern der Maßstab für die Zukunft, wie ein Château Bordeaux auszusehen habe. Umso überraschender der Kommentar der siegreichen Architekten Dillon und de Gastines: „Wir ließen uns durch die architektenlose Architektur des Médoc inspirieren und wollten zunächst einmal ein Gleichgewicht zwischen den drei Komponenten Weinberg, Château und Chai herstellen". Ihr Trick war einfach: das Motiv der Mauer „verlängern, die sich manchmal zum Tor, Eckpfeiler oder Skulptur verwandelt".

The eternal classic | It was surely one of the most exciting phases in modern architecture when a decision was reached to hold the "Chateau Pichon-Longueville" competition in 1988. This was no ordinary building, but a standard which would be used in the future to determine what a Bordeaux chateau should look like. It therefore came as even more of a surprise to hear the comment made by the winning architects, Dillon and de Gastines: "We let ourselves be inspired by the architect-free architecture of the Médoc and we wanted first of all to create an equilibrium between the three components, vineyard, chateau and chai". Their trick was simple: "to extend (the wall motif), which sometimes transforms itself into a gateway, corner pillar or sculpture".

Le classique éternel | On se trouvait certainement dans une phase excitante de l'architecture moderne lorsque le concours pour le Château Pichon-Longueville a été lancé en 1988. Il ne s'agissait pas d'un bâtiment quelconque: il devait déterminer l'apparence d'un Château bordelais pour l'avenir. Le commentaire des architectes lauréats Dillon et de Gastines est d'autant plus surprenant: "Nous nous sommes inspirés de l'architecture sans architectes du Médoc et voulions avant tout établir un équilibre entre les trois composants: vignoble, château et chai". Leur parti était simple: prolonger le thème du mur "qui se transforme parfois en portail, en poteau d'angle ou en sculpture".

[1]

Dieses Konzept der Rücksichtnahme und Zurückhaltung wurde dann aber in Zeichnung, Modell und Rohbau zu einem Festival plastischer Vielfalt: Das Château selbst doppelt sich virtuell in der Wasserfläche eines zentralen Beckens, der Weinberg wird durch eine sanft geneigte Freitreppe über den Dächern der Empfangs- und Probierräume erschlossen – in einer Art, wie sie sonst Volkstribunen für sich reklamieren.

The drawing, model and shell of the building, however, turned this concept into a festival of three-dimensional variety: the chateau itself is mirrored, and thereby virtually doubled, in the surface of a central pond, the vineyard is accessible by a gently inclined flight of steps leading above the roofs of the reception and tasting rooms – in a manner normally claimed by tribunes as their own.

Ce concept, basé sur la modestie et le respect de l'existant, a ensuite été transformé à travers dessins, maquettes et construction en un festival de variations plastiques. Le Château est virtuellement doublé grâce au miroir d'eau d'un bassin central. Le vignoble est accessible grâce à un escalier extérieur à la pente douce, disposé au-dessus du toit de l'accueil et des salles de dégustation, un peu comme des tribunes populaires.

Vorherige Seiten: Ansicht des neuen Kellergebäudes mit dem sogenannten „Fenster zum Himmel" (Zustand 1992) [1] Panoramafoto mit altem Schloß Pichon-Longueville und Neubau des Kellergebäudes (Zustand 1992)

Previous pages: view of the new cellar building with its so-called "window to Heaven" (from 1992) [1] Panorama photo with the old Pichon-Longueville chateau and the new cellar building (from 1992)

Pages précédentes: vue du nouveau bâtiment des caves avec la "fenêtre sur le ciel" (situation en 1992) [1] Vue panoramique avec l'ancien Château Pichon-Longueville et le nouveau bâtiment des caves (situation en 1992)

[1]

Doch das Monumentale hat sich bis heute buchstäblich verwachsen. Heute ist das neue Château Pichon-Longueville ein Ort der Selbstverständlichkeit und der Kontinuität. Natürliche Alterung des Betons, rankender Wein und gewachsene Bäume garantieren dies. Und die wechselnden Lichterstimmungen der Wasserlandschaft zwischen Atlantik und Gironde tun ihr übriges dazu. Selbst das markante offene Portal mit zwei flankierenden Obelisken oberhalb des Cuvier- und Chai-Zugangs, ein sogenanntes „Fenster zum Himmel", wie es Besitzer Jean Michel Cazes nennt, wirkt heute wie der logische Salut, den der Neubau dem Altbau einfach schuldig ist. Kleingebilde aus Kruzifix, Turm und Skulptur haben im Médoc ohnehin eine lange Tradition.

Today the new Chateau Pichon-Longueville is a place of naturalness and continuity. The natural ageing of the concrete, the climbing wine and the trees now grown guarantee this. And the changing atmosphere of light of the watery landscape between the Atlantic and Gironde does the rest. Even the prominent, open portal flanked by two obelisks above the entrance to the cuvier and chai - a so-called "window to Heaven" as the owner Jean Michel Cazes termed it - today appears, as a modern building, to be logically saluting the old as if it simply owed this to it. Small buildings with crucifix, tower and sculpture have a long tradition in the Médoc anyway.

Le nouveau Château Pichon-Longueville est aujourd'hui un lieu d'évidence et de continuité. Le vieillissement naturel du béton, la vigne vierge et les arbres qui ont grandi ont littéralement recouvert son caractère monumental. La luminosité changeante du paysage maritime entre Atlantique et Gironde fait le reste. Même le majestueux portail flanqué de deux obélisques, qui marque l'accès au cuvier et au chai et que le propriétaire Jean Michel Cazes nomme "fenêtre sur le ciel", apparaît aujourd'hui comme un salut logique dont le nouveau bâtiment est redevable à l'ancien. Crucifix, tours ou sculptures, les petites constructions ont dans le Médoc une longue tradition.

[2]

[3]

[1] „Fenster zum Himmel": Skulpturale Kleinarchitektur hat im Médoc Tradition
[2] Neben der zentralen Achse auf das alte Schloß wurde quer dazu eine zweite von der Freitreppe auf den Keller mit dem „Fenster zum Himmel" inszeniert
[3] Mauerdetail mit "Schnecke"

[1] "Window to Heaven": the Médoc has a tradition of sculptural, detailed architecture
[2] A second axis was created by the stairs to the cellar with its "window to Heaven" at right angles to the central axis on which the old chateau lies
[3] Wall detail with "snail"

[1] "Fenêtre sur le ciel": les petites constructions sculpturales ont dans le Médoc une longue tradition
[2] Perpendiculairement à l'axe central vers le vieux château, un deuxième axe reliant l'escalier extérieur à la cave a été mis en scène avec la "fenêtre sur le ciel"
[3] Détail du mur avec une des volutes

[1]

Innen im Cuvier wird die Architektur nun endgültig zum Theater des Weines, allerdings viel offensiver als auf „Lafite". Die Besucher sind geladene Zuschauer einer beinahe „heiligen" Handlung: der Pflege und Bearbeitung eines großen Bordeaux-Weines. Sie werden auf eine runde Galerie geführt und schauen wie aus Logen hinunter in den Cuvier. Hier gibt es nur noch Blickkontakt: Tourismus und Wein behindern sich nicht mehr, nicht einmal in den turbulenten Tagen der Ernte. Licht fällt auf eine Bühnenrotunde zwischen schräg gestellten Säulen, von denen niemand so recht weiß, ob sie nicht gleich einknicken. Sie tun es natürlich nicht. Sondern sie dienen einer dramatischen Inszenierung.

Inside in the cuvier the architecture now finally becomes a theatre of wine, albeit much more offensive than that at "Lafite". The visitors are spectators invited to witness an almost "holy" act: the cultivation and processing of a great Bordeaux wine. They are led onto a round gallery and look down, as if from theatre boxes, into the cuvier. Here there is only eye contact – tourism and wine no longer hinder each other, not even in the turbulent days of the grape harvest. Light falls onto a stage rotunda between obliquely positioned columns; no-one knows for sure whether these are going to give way at any moment. Obviously they don't. Rather they act as a dramatic stage setting.

A l'intérieur, dans le cuvier, l'architecture devient définitivement, et d'une manière beaucoup plus affirmée qu'à Lafite, le théâtre du vin. Les visiteurs sont des spectateurs invités à un acte presque "sacré": les soins et les traitements apportés à un grand Bordeaux. A partir d'une galerie circulaire qui rappelle les loges d'un théâtre, ils regardent en bas dans le cuvier. Ici, le contact n'est que visuel: tourisme et production ne se gênent plus, même pas pendant la période turbulente de la récolte. La lumière tombe sur une scène circulaire, rotonde entourée de poteaux inclinés, dont on se demande s'ils ne vont pas se briser dans l'instant. Ils ne le font pas, bien sûr: ils participent seulement à une mise en scène dramatique.

Vorherige Seiten: Die Freitreppe führt in die Weinberge und wird zum Dach für die Degustations- und Empfangsräume
[1] „Theater des Weins": mit Stützen, die bewußt schräg gestellt wurden
[2] Kunst und Wein: Selbst die Tanks im Cuvier wirken wie ausgesuchte Skulpturen

Previous pages: the flight of steps leads into the vineyards and turns into the roof of the tasting and reception areas
[1] "Theatre of wine": with supports deliberately positioned at an oblique angle
[2] Art and wine: even the tanks in the cuvier have the air of exquisite sculptures

Pages précédentes: l'escalier extérieur mène dans les vignes et devient toiture au-dessus de l'espace d'accueil et des salons de dégustation
[1] Le "théâtre du vin", avec des colonnes volontairement disposées en oblique
[2] L'art et le vin : même les cuves du cuvier ressemblent à des sculptures

[1]

Vorherige Seiten: Die
Architekten gaben jeder
Säule im Chai ein unter-
schiedliches Kapitell
[1-2] Abendstimmung
über Pichon-Longuevil-
le: Die Dorfstraße führt
direkt durch die Anla-
gen des Weinguts

Previous pages: the
architects gave each of
the columns in the chai a
different capital
[1-2] Evening falls over
Pichon-Longueville: the
village road runs directly
through the estate

Pages précédentes: les
architectes ont donné à
chaque colonne du chai
un chapiteau différent
[1-2] Soleil couchant
sur Pichon-Longueville:
la rue du village traver-
se les installations du
domaine

Der Wettbewerb   The Competition

1

Im August 1988 gewannen die Architekten Dillon und de Gastines den Architekturwettbewerb für die Neubauten auf Pichon-Longueville. Die Wettbewerbszeichnung (1) zeigt die klassizistische Strenge der Anlage mit einer Hauptblickachse, die von der Straße über ein Wasserbecken auf das Schloß gelegt ist. Links liegen Empfang, Büros und Probierräume. Sie finden teilweise unter der Freitreppe Platz, die zu den Weinbergen und Parkplätzen führt.

In August 1988 the architects, Dillon and de Gastines, won the architecture prize for the new buildings on the Pichon-Longueville estate. The drawing submitted (1) shows the classical austerity of the estate with a central axis running across the street and over a pool towards the chateau. To the left are the reception, office and tasting areas. These were partially incorporated into the area below the flight of steps leading to the vineyards and car parks. On the right side of the

En août 1988, les architectes Dillon et de Gastines ont gagné le concours d'architecture pour les nouvelles constructions du domaine Pichon-Longueville. Le projet du concours (1) montre la rigueur classique du domaine avec un axe visuel principal partant de la rue et dirigé vers le château en passant au-dessus d'un bassin. Chai et cuvier sont placés à droite de l'axe ; à gauche se trouvent l'accueil, les bureaux et les salons de dégustation, situés en partie sous l'escalier menant aux vign-

Le concours

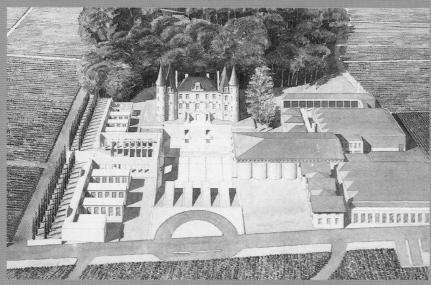

2

3

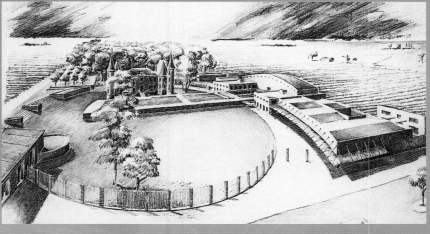

Auf der rechten Seite der Anlage: Chai und Cuvier. Die beiden unteren Fotos zeigen das sogenannte „Theater des Weins" im Rohbau und im heutigen Zustand.

Auch die beiden anderen Architektengruppen befleißigten sich strenger, ja traditioneller Gliederung und Gruppierung der Neubauten, beide stellten das Schloß in den optischen Mittelpunkt. Doch weder den Spaniern Ustarroz und Iniguez (2) noch dem Pariser Montes (3) gelang es, die großen Neubaumaße so geschickt zu integrieren und so selbstverständlich zum Teil der Landschaft werden zu lassen wie den Siegerarchitekten.

estate: chai and cuvier. The two photos below show the so-called "theatre of wine" as a shell of a building and as it stands today.

The other two groups also endeavoured to arrange and group the new buildings in a traditional way, both having the chateau as the central focal point. And yet neither the Spaniards, Ustarroz and Iniguez (2) nor the Parisian, Montes (3) were as successful as the winning architects in integrating the large dimensions of the new buildings so skilfully and incorporating them so naturally into the landscape.

obles et à l'aire de stationnement. Les deux photographies en bas de page montrent le "théâtre du vin" au cours du chantier et dans son état actuel.

Les deux autres équipes d'architectes participant au concours ont répondu avec la même rigueur et une organisation traditionnelle des nouvelles installations, plaçant pareillement le château au centre de la composition. Cependant, ni les espagnols Ustarroz et Iniguez (2), ni le parisien Montes (3) ne sont arrivés aussi adroitement que l'équipe retenue à intégrer le programme important des nouveaux bâtiments de manière naturelle dans le paysage.

Jean Miche

Im Zusammenhang mit der Ausschreibung 1990 für Pichon-Longueville sprachen Sie von einem klassischen Schloß für das 3. Jahrtausend. Heute, nach zehn Jahren, frage ich Sie, ob Sie dieses Ziel verwirklicht sehen. Oder gibt es andere Kriterien, mit denen Sie Pichon-Longueville charakterisieren würden?

Interview

Ich denke, daß sich das Pichon-Longueville Projekt nach rund 10 Jahren gut in die Landschaft eingefügt hat. Das war unser Ziel und auch der Hauptgrund für unsere architektonische Entscheidung. Heute – und hoffentlich noch lange – gehört der Bau zu dieser wunderschönen Umgebung der Weinberge St. Lambert - St. Julien. Für mich ist der Bau außerdem ein Zeuge für die Epoche, in der er gebaut wurde: Eine Epoche geprägt von schnellem technischen Wachstum und von gesteigertem Selbstbewußtsein – ja vom Stolz – der Weingüter im Bordeaux. Er soll ein Symbol sein für die hohe Qualität des Weinbaus.

Heute sind die Bordeaux-Weine die exklusivsten und teuersten der ganzen Welt. Besonders das Médoc-Gebiet ist eine Garantie für hohe Qualität und großen Erfolg. Welche Rolle spielt die Architektur dabei?

Die Architektur spielt keine direkte Rolle für die Weinproduktion, vermittelt aber einen bestimmten Esprit. In unserem Fall ist die Architektur ein Bild und zeigt nach außen unseren Willen, immer besser darin werden zu wollen, beste Weine zu produzieren und gleichzeitig diese historische Gegend zu respektieren, von der wir nur die temporären Nutznießer sind. Andere werden nach uns kommen, wir wollen hoffen, daß das, was wir gebaut haben, eine Richtlinie für die sein wird.

Glauben Sie, daß der Erfolg der Bordeaux-Weine weiteren Ausbau erfordert – vielleicht sogar neue Gebäude? Erwarten Sie, daß sich die Architektursprache dann ändern wird?

Ich kann nicht sagen, ob es viele neue Bauten im Bordeaux geben wird. In Pichon hatten wir die große Chance, uns mit dem Anwesen in einem Moment beschäftigen zu können, in dem sich das Weingut in seiner historischen Entwicklung ein bißchen Ruhe gönnte. So was ist selten im Bordeaux, immer seltener.

Auf jeden Fall ist jetzt in Pichon das Wichtigste getan. Vielleicht werden wir bald andere Projekte angehen. Was die Architektursprache betrifft, so bin ich mir sicher, daß sie den „Spirit" ihrer Epoche immer auf sehr direkte Art ausdrückt. Das bedingt stetige Veränderung. Die guten Projekte sind innovativ. Und alles ändert sich heutzutage sehr schnell. Ich würde mich freuen, wieder mit einer ähnlichen Herausforderung konfrontiert zu werden (z.B. wie mit unserem Weingut Disznokö in Ungarn, wo wir, meiner Meinung nach, einen herausragenden Bau hingestellt haben). Aber wahrscheinlich käme dann eine andere Lösung heraus als vor zehn Jahren.

Within the context of the 1990 competition for Pichon-Longueville you spoke of a classical chateau for the 3rd millennium. Today, almost ten years later, I would like to ask you if you feel that this objective has been realised. Or are there other means for you to characterise Pichon-Longueville?

I think that the Pichon-Longueville project adapted itself well into the countryside after about 10 years. That was our goal and the main reason for our architectonic decision. Today, and hopefully for a long time yet, the building will belong to these beautiful surroundings of the St Lambert-St Julien. Apart from that the building is a witness to the epoch in which it has been built: An epoch that was influenced by fast technical growth and by increased self-confidence – indeed, by pride – for the wine estates in Bordeaux. It is meant to be a symbol of the high quality of the vineyards.

Today, Bordeaux wines are the most exclusive and precious worldwide. Especially the Médoc area is evenly a promise of high quality and great success. Which role plays the architecture for this success?

The architecture does not play a direct role in the production of wine. However, it conveys a certain esprit. In our case the architecture is a picture that shows our intentions to the outside world: a will to constantly improve, to produce wine of a high quality, and at the same time, to shows that we respect this historic region which we are using temporarily. Others will come after us and we hope that what we have built up will be used as a guideline for others.

Do you think that the success of Bordeaux wines might allow further expansion and maybe even a new building? Do you expect the architectural language to alter?

I can't say whether there will be many new buildings in the Bordeaux. In Pichon we had a real opportunity to deal with the estate at a time in which the wine estate was still in its historic development. Such a thing is rare in Bordeaux – and it is becoming rarer and rarer. In any case the most important thing has been achieved in Pichon. Perhaps we'll tackle other projects soon. When it comes to the architectural language, I'm sure that it always expresses the spirit of its epoch. And this continually changes and grows. I would look forward to being confronted with a similar challenge (e.g. as with our wine estate in Disznokö Hungary, where we have, in my opinion, placed a building that stands out). But this would probably have resulted in another solution ten years ago.

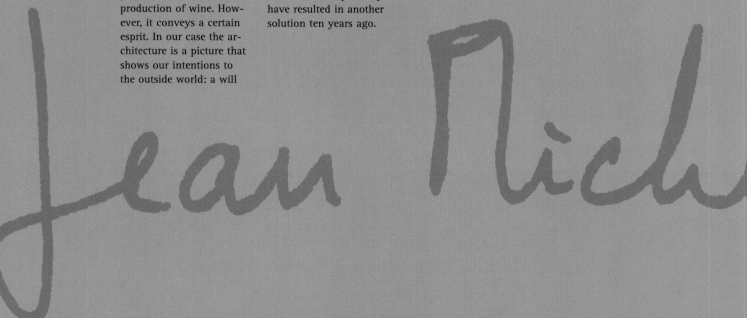

En 1990, lors du lancement du concours pour Pichon-Longueville, vous avez parlé d'un Château classique pour le 3ème millénaire. Aujourd'hui, dix ans après, pensez-vous que ce but ait été atteint ? Et pourriez-vous caractériser Pichon-Longueville avec d'autres critères ?

Je pense que le projet de Pichon-Longueville, qui a près de 10 ans, est maintenant bien inscrit dans le paysage. Il était conçu pour cela et ce fut la raison essentielle de notre choix architectural. Aujourd'hui, et pour longtemps, il fait partie de ce décor exceptionnel du plateau de vignobles de St Lambert - St Julien. C'est aussi pour moi un témoin de l'époque à laquelle il a été construit, qui était une époque d'évolution technique rapide, de montée en puissance du vignoble bordelais, et même de fierté. C'est aussi un signal fort du renouveau de la propriété, et un symbole de la qualité du travail viticole et vinicole qui a été entrepris à ce moment-là.

Aujourd'hui, les vins de Bordeaux sont les plus exceptionnels et les plus chers du monde. La région du Médoc, en particulier, représente une garantie de haute qualité et de grand succès. Quel rôle joue l'architecture dans ce domaine ?

L'architecture ne joue pas de rôle dans la vinification proprement dite, mais elle traduit un état d'esprit. Dans notre cas, l'architecture est une image, et représente à l'extérieur l'effort que nous réalisons pour faire toujours mieux, plus dépouillé, classique, pour élaborer des vins de haut niveau, sans concession aux modes, en respectant le terroir historique dont nous sommes temporairement les dépositaires. D'autres viendront après nous, et nous espérons que ce que nous avons édifié sera pour eux comme une sorte de message et une ligne de conduite.

Croyez-vous que le succès du vin de Bordeaux nécessite des agrandissements supplémentaires, peut-être même de nouveaux bâtiments ? Attendez-vous que le vocabulaire architectural soit alors différent ?

Je ne sais pas si Bordeaux connaîtra beaucoup de nouvelles constructions dans les années à venir. Nous avons eu à Pichon la très grande chance de nous intéresser à une propriété à un moment où elle avait pris beaucoup de retard dans son évolution historique. Une telle situation est rare à Bordeaux, de plus en plus rare. En tous cas, pour nous, à Pichon, l'essentiel est fait. Nous aurons peut-être ailleurs d'autres projets. Quand au langage architectural, je suis persuadé qu'il interprète toujours l'esprit de son époque de façon très directe. Donc, il évolue en permanence. Les bons projets sont originaux. Et tout change aujourd'hui très vite. Je serais pour ma part vraiment très heureux d'être une autre fois confronté à un challenge comme celui que nous avons eu à Pichon (ou à Disznokö en Hongrie, où nous avons aussi construit, en 1997, une installation superbe - à mon avis). Mais je pense que la réponse serait différente, car nous voudrions exprimer une époque et des préoccupations qui ne sont plus tout à fait les mêmes sur un certain nombre de questions.

Château
Lynch-Bages

Weißes Gebirge | Das Château Lynch-Bages ist seit dem Jahr 1934 im Besitz der für die Fachkompetenz für Weinbau bekannten Familie Cazes. 1974 übernahm Jean Michel Cazes die Aufgabe, das Gut neu zu strukturieren; er ist auch für das benachbarte Château Pichon-Longueville zuständig. Lynch-Bages zählt zu den großen, aber unauffälligen, jedoch in der Funktion vorzüglich angelegten Gütern. Ein Teil der sehr alten Anlagen ist inzwischen stillgelegt, wie der ursprüngliche Bereich mit Presse und Gärkeller. Er ist allerdings heute als kleines Museum immer noch zu besichtigen. Noch vor einigen Jahren stand in Sichtweite eine wirklich häßliche Lagerhalle. Jetzt faltet sich dort ein Gebirge aus hellem Metall auf. Hier wird der Weißwein M. Lynch auf Flaschen abgefüllt und gelagert. Die Architektur ist kongenial zur Klasse des weißen Bordeaux und ein Beispiel dafür, daß Lagerhallen nicht mehr häßlich sein müssen und sich auch aufwendige und auffällige Architektur ins liebliche Médoc einpassen läßt.

White mountains | Since 1934 the Lynch-Bages chateau has been owned by the Cazes family, known for their expert competence in wine-growing. In 1974 Jean Michel Cazes took over the task of restructuring the estate; he is also responsible for the neighbouring chateau, "Pichon-Longueville". Lynch-Bages is one of the larger, though inconspicuous, estates, superbly laid out from a functional point of view. Part of the very old estate has since been closed down, as has the original area housing a press and fermentation cellar. However, it can still be visited today as a small museum. A few years ago a very ugly warehouse was still visible. Now a mountain of light metal unfolds here. It is here that the white wine M. Lynch is bottled and stored. The architecture is congenial to the class of that white Bordeaux and is living proof that warehouses no longer have to be ugly, and that elaborate and conspicuous architecture can blend in with the lovely Médoc scenery.

Blanches collines | Le Château Lynch-Bages est depuis 1934 dans les mains de la famille Cazes, connue pour ses compétences dans le domaine vinicole. Jean Michel Cazes, qui est aussi responsable du Château voisin, Pichon-Longueville, a entrepris en 1974 la restructuration du domaine Lynch-Bages, aménagé de manière remarquablement fonctionnelle. Il compte parmi les grands domaines mais reste discret. Trop anciennes, certaines parties des installations, comme le pressoir et le cuvier d'origine, ne sont plus en service. Un petit musée y a été aménagé. Il y a quelques années, un entrepôt vraiment très laid était encore visible à proximité. Aujourd'hui, des collines en métal clair y sont déployées. C'est là que l'on met en bouteilles et que l'on entrepose l'excellent vin blanc M. Lynch du domaine. L'architecture est de la même classe que ce Bordeaux blanc. Ce bâtiment prouve que les entrepôts ne doivent pas toujours être affreux et qu'une construction luxueuse et voyante peut s'intégrer dans le paysage charmant du Médoc.

[1]

[2]

[1] Endpunkt jeder Be-
sichtigung: die festliche
Degustation
[2] Fast unendlich: der
Weinkeller
[3] Eingepaßt: Die Archi-
tektur ist traditionell
[4] Museal: Der Cuvier
des 19. Jahrhunderts
wurde stillgelegt, aber
erhalten
[5] und nachfolgende
Seiten: blitzendes
Hallengebirge für den
Weißwein M. Lynch

[1] The end of any visit:
tasting the wine
[2] Almost never-ending:
the wine cellar
[3] Blending in: the
architecture is traditional
[4] Museum: the cuvier
was closed in the 19th
Century, but preserved
[5] and following pages:
gleaming mountain of
halls for the M. Lynch
white wine

[1] Fin de la visite: la
dégustation
[2] Presque infinie: la
cave à vin
[3] Adaptation: l'archi-
tecture est traditionnelle
[4] Muséographie: le
cuvier du 19ème siècle
n'est plus en service,
mais il a été conservé
[5] et pages suivantes:
des collines métalliques
scintillantes pour le vin
blanc M. Lynch

[3]

[4]

[5]

Château Branaire

Ruhe und Sturm | Branaire bei St. Julien ist eine Oase französischer Adelsromantik: Das Château und seine feingliedrigen Nebenbauten rahmen kleine Gartenhöfe und Alleen ein. Irgendwo – ob innen in den gepflegten Salons oder draußen an den Buchsbäumen – irgendwo wird immer gerade gewerkelt, gepinselt, restauriert und gepflanzt. Ein Ambiente der Tradition und Ruhe.

Als hier 1990 aus önologischen und betriebswirtschaftlichen Gründen erweitert werden mußte, galt für die Architekten der Familie Mazieres das Gesetz, außen dieses perfekte Ensemble nicht zu stören. Mit flachen Dächern, pastellfarbenen Wänden und großer Zurückhaltung gehorchten sie dem Diktat freiwillig und perfekt. Sogar die Karikatur eines prächtigen Säulenportals vor der Einfahrt zum Cuvier wirkt passend gemütlich. Gemessen an der expressiven Gestaltungswucht eines Michael Graves im Napa Valley ist dies alles einfach und harmlos.

Calm and storm | Branaire near St. Julien is an oasis of French noble romanticism: small gardens and avenues are framed by the chateau and its slender annexes. Somewhere - whether within in the stylish salons or outside by the box trees – somewhere there is always someone pottering about, something being painted, restored or planted. An ambience of tradition and serenity reigns.

When, in 1990, the estate had to be extended for oenologic reasons as well as reasons connected with the management of the business, a law was set down for the architects of the Mazieres family, dictating that this perfect ensemble should not be destroyed. With flat roofs, pastel-coloured walls and a great deal of restraint, they obeyed this dictate voluntarily and in perfect fashion. Even the caricature of a magnificent columned portal in front of the entrance to the cuvier has a suitably "comfortable" feel. Measured against the expressive creative power of a Michael Graves in the Napa Valley, all of this is simple and harmless.

Calme et tempête | Branaire, près de St. Julien, est une oasis de la noblesse romantique française. Le Château et ses dépendances composent un ensemble bâti découpé d'allées et de petites cours. Á l'intérieur, dans les salons soignés, ou dehors, près des buis taillés, il y a toujours quelqu'un qui est en train de bricoler, de peindre, de restaurer ou de jardiner. L'ambiance sereine est chargée de tradition.

Lorsque pour des raisons œnologiques et logistiques on a dû agrandir le domaine en 1990, la famille Mazieres a demandé à ses architectes de ne pas détruire l'aspect extérieur de cet ensemble harmonieux. Avec des toits en terrasse et des façades aux tons pastels, ceux-ci ont répondu avec pertinence et modestie à cette injonction. Même la caricature d'un majestueux portail à colonnes devant l'entrée du cuvier est agréablement débonnaire. Comparé à la violence expressive d'un Michael Graves à Napa valley, tout cela semble discret et anodin.

[1]

Anders, ja ganz anders, innen. Der längliche Chai wirkt auch hier wie ein „Andachtsraum": Dafür sorgen beispielsweise Kassettendecken und die mit Beton gefüllten Stahlsäulen und deren konische Kapitelle. Einen allerdings ganz anderen Charakter erhielt der zweigeschossige Cuvier. Dank seiner Hanglage war hier wieder das Prinzip der Traubenanlieferung von oben möglich, unten stehen die Tanks und genau in der Mitte (wiederum oben) ein vieleckiger Glaspavillon; er wirkt wie die Kommandozentrale einer Autofabrik. Stahlfachwerkträger auf denen das große Dach ruht, betonen zusätzlich den Fabrikcharakter des Raums: sicher eine deftige Überraschung für jeden, der draußen noch an Schloßgeister und Matinees unter Palmen dachte.

It is different, yes very different, inside. The long, narrow chai here also takes on the appearance of a place of worship: there are cassette ceilings, for example, and steel pillars filled with concrete with conical capitals. The double-level cuvier has a completely different character. Thanks to its being situated on a slope, the principle of delivering the grapes from above was again possible; the tanks stand below, and in the exact centre (again above) is a polygonal glass pavilion with the appearance of a car factory command post. Steel beams on which the large roof rests further emphasise the factory-like character of the room: certainly a big surprise for anyone who was still entertaining thoughts of ghosts and matinees under palm trees outside.

L'intérieur, lui, est bien différent. Tout en longueur, avec un plafond à caissons et des colonnes en acier remplies de béton surmontées de chapiteaux coniques, le chai ressemble à un sanctuaire. Le cuvier à deux étages a un tout autre caractère. Sa situation dans la pente du terrain favorise l'application d'un principe éprouvé: livraison du raisin à l'étage supérieur, citernes au niveau bas. Un pavillon vitré polygonal en position centrale évoque le poste de commandes d'une usine automobile. La nappe tridimensionelle en acier sur laquelle repose le grand toit souligne encore le caractère industriel de l'espace. C'est une surprise de taille pour celui qui rêvait encore à l'extérieur des fantômes du château ou d'un Martini sous les palmiers.

[2]

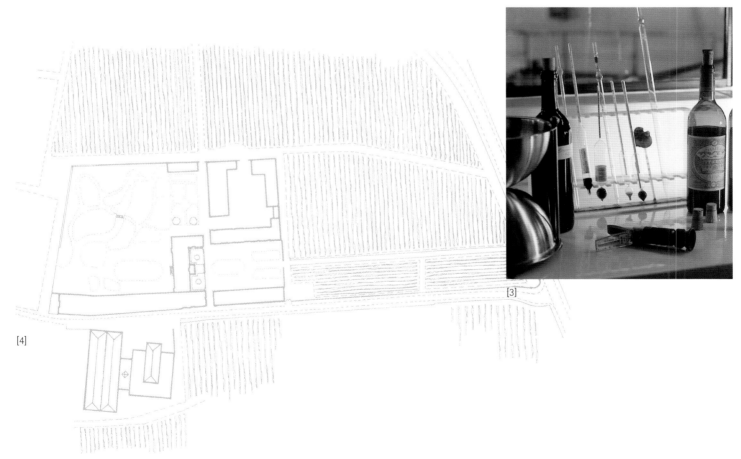

[3]

[4]

[3] Es ist angerichtet – zur Probe kostbarer Weine
[4] Gesamtübersicht; die Neubauten sind in der Zeichnung zu finden

[3] The wine is served – sumptuous wines to taste
[4] Overall view; the new buildings can be found in the lower drawing

[3] Tout est prêt pour la dégustation de vins précieux
[4] Vue d'ensemble : les nouvelles installations se trouvent dans la partie du dessin

[1]

[3]

[2]

[4]

[1+5] Kontrast zum
Cuvier: Im rechteckigen
Chai herrscht andachts-
volle Stimmung
[3] Schnitt durch den
zweigeschossigen
Cuvier
[2+4] Zwischenspiel:
Vorbereitungen für die
Degustation

[1+5] Contrast to the
cuvier: a reverent atmos-
phere pervades the rec-
tangular chai
[3] Section between the
double-level cuvier
[2+4] Interlude: prepar-
ing for the tasting

[1+5] Contraste avec le
cuvier: dans le chai rec-
tangulaire, une ambian-
ce de recueillement do-
mine
[3] Coupe à travers le
cuvier de deux étages
[2+4] Intermède: prépa-
ration pour la dégusta-
tion

Domaines Henry Martin

Sanfter Aufstand in der Dorfstraße |

Wenn man nicht aufpaßt, ist das Auto schon vorbeigefahren. Eine neue, aber unauffällige Betonwand verlängert den trivialen Altbaubestand des Weindorfes Beychevelle. Erst der Blick nach oben trifft eine hier überraschende Dachwelle, die über dem Staffelgeschoß dahinfließt. Die runde Hausecke besteht aus Metall und wurde als klare Referenz an die Gärtanks eines Weingutes angelegt. Die Domaines Henry Martin (mit ihren Marken Château Gloria und Château Saint-Pierre) haben hier im Dörfchen ihren Weinkeller und das Besucherzentrum (hoch oben unter der Dachwelle) untergebracht. DHM ist eines der wenigen Beispiele dafür, wie ein Weingut als kompaktes Haus mitten ins Dorf zu stellen ist. Und es gelang. Vorbildlich ist die Integration ins Dorfbild, die Betonwand tut in ihrer ganzen Sprödigkeit so, als wäre sie so alt wie die herumstehenden Putzhäuschen.

Quite rebellion in the village street |

If not enough attention is paid, it is easy to drive straight past the estate. A new, yet inconspicuous, concrete wall extends the continuance of the old buildings belonging to the wine village, Beychevelle. First, on looking upwards, the visitor's gaze is met by a surprising wave-like roof, flowing onto the step-like levels. The round corner of the house is made of metal and clearly represents the fermentation tanks of an estate. The wine cellars of Domaines Henry Martin (with its makes, Château Gloria and Château Saint-Pierre) are accommodated here in the small village, as is the visitor's centre (high up under the wave-like roof). DHM is one of the few examples of how an estate can be positioned like a compact house in the centre of the village. And it worked. The integration of the estate into the character of the village is exemplary; the concrete wall in all its roughness appears to be as old as the was houses around it.

Intégration douce dans une rue de village |

Si l'on ne fait pas attention, la voiture a déjà dépassé le domaine avant qu'on l'aperçoive. Un mur en béton, neuf mais discret, prolonge le banal bâti existant du village viticole de Beychevelle. C'est seulement en levant la tête que l'on remarque une surprenante toiture ondulée qui flotte au dessus de l'étage supérieur. Réalisé en métal, l'angle arrondi du bâtiment est une référence évidente aux citernes de fermentation. Les Domaines Henry Martin, avec leurs crus Château Gloria et Château Saint-Pierre, ont construit dans ce petit village leur cave et un centre d'accueil pour les visiteurs, disposé tout en haut, sous la vague de la toiture. DHM démontre qu'un domaine viticole peut aussi être un bâtiment compact situé au centre d'un village. Et c'est réussi! L'intégration dans l'environnement bâti est exemplaire. Le mur en béton, par sa rugosité, donne l'impression qu'il est aussi vieux que les petites maisons couvertes de crépi qui l'entourent.

[1]

Ein interessanter Einfall sind die runden Luken, die es gestatten, von innen aus dem Weinkeller herauszuschauen. Auf der Rückseite sorgen rauhe Holzbalken und verzinkter Stahl für den in Mode gekommenen Schäbi-Schick. Hier allerdings paßt er gut her.

Das Haus ist nach dem Prinzip organisiert: „unten ruht und reift der Wein" und „oben wird er dann probiert" . Die Besucher werden eine beeindruckende, einläufige Treppe hinaufgeschickt, um dann an einer restaurierten Bar aus den dreißiger Jahren die Kreationen des Hauses zu schmecken, zu prüfen und zu probieren. Von dort kann auch der Blick hinunter ins friedliche Dorf schweifen, wo man nicht ahnt, daß hinter grauen Mauern eine sanfte architektonische Gestaltungsrevolution stattfindet.

The round skylights, allowing a view out of the wine cellar, are an interesting idea. To the rear, rough wooden beams and galvanised steel create a fashionable shabby-chic effect. It fits in well here, though.

The house is organised according to the following principle: "the wine rests and matures below" and "then it is tasted above". The visitors are sent up an impressive, worn stairway to then taste and test the creations of the house at a restored thirties-style bar. From here one's gaze can roam to the serene village where it's impossible to guess that a peaceful, architectonic, creative revolution is taking place behind grey walls.

Idée intéressante: des ouvertures rondes permettent de regarder depuis le cellier vers l'extérieur. Sur l'arrière, des poutres en bois brut de sciage et de l'acier galvanisé sacrifient à la mode minimaliste. Dans ce contexte, c'est assez approprié.

Le bâtiment est organisé selon le principe: "en bas, le vin repose et mûrit"; "en haut, il est dégusté". Les visiteurs gagnent l'étage en empruntant l'unique volée d'un escalier large et imposant qui les mène à un bar des années 30 où ils peuvent humer, goûter et déguster les créations de la Maison. De là, le regard peut glisser vers le paisible village où personne n'imagine que derrière des murs gris une douce révolution de la conception architecturale a eu lieu.

Vorherige Seiten: Revolutionäre Neubauten im Altbaubestand: Gesamtansicht mit Eingang und Dachwelle
[1] Hingucker: Interessante Details aus dem Eingangsbereich
[2] Temperaturanzeige im Altbau

Previous pages: revolutionary new buildings added on to the old: overall view with entrance and wave-like roof
[1] Looking on: details of the entrance area
[2] Temperature indicator in the old building

Pages précédentes: de nouvelles constructions révolutionnaires au milieu du bâti existant – vue générale avec l'entrée et la vague de la toiture
[1] Détails de l'entrée
[2] Indication de la température dans le bâtiment ancien

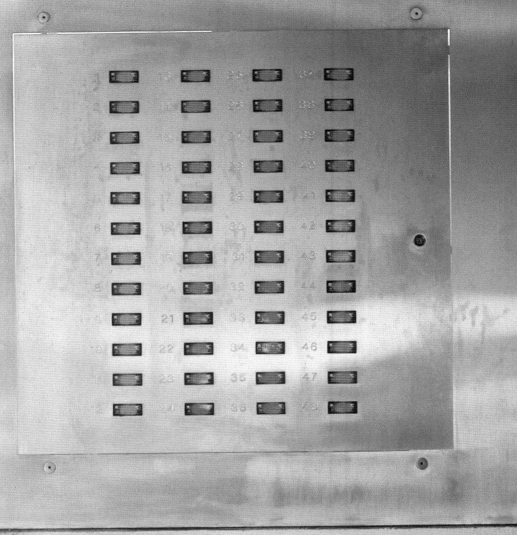

DOMAINES HENRI MARTIN

[1]

[2]

[3]

[1-2] Totale und Detail der Bar für die Degustation; sie stammt aus den dreißiger Jahren
[3] Mutig und modern wie die Fassade: Stufen und Geländer der Weinkeller-Treppe

[1-2] The complete bar, used for wine tasting, with detail; the bar originates from the thirties
[3] Bold and modern like the facade: steps and banister of the wine cellar

[1-2] Vue d'ensemble et détail du bar de dégustation, qui date des années 30
[3] Courageux et moderne comme les façades : les marches et le garde-corps de l'escalier de la cave à vin

Château d'Arsac

Der Code heißt Blau | Als 1986 das Château d'Arsac wieder eröffnet wurde, blieben Wohnhaus, Gärkeller und Remise erhalten; das heißt ihre Mauern. Die alten Holztüren ersetzte Architekt Patrick Hernandez durch silbern glänzende Aluminiumpaneele, drinnen inszenierte er aus Stahl und Blech eine High-Tech-Welt, und den neuen Anbau für einen Lagerkeller krönte er mit einem zackigen Dach. Es wirkt gerade hier im Bordeaux fast bizarr, wenn die alten Sandsteinfassaden im Spiegelglas der Neubauten zu Zerrbildern werden. Auch wenn dies auf den ersten Blick wie die Mischung aus Cru Bordeaux und Fast Food daherkommt, hat Hernandez die Regeln und auch die Bestandteile des önologischen Produktionsprozesses beachtet und eine perfekt funktionierende Struktur entworfen.

Blue is the code | When the Château d'Arsac was reopened in 1986, the residential building, fermentation cellar and outbuilding were preserved; that is to say their walls. The architect, Patrick Hernandez, replaced the old wooden doors with gleaming silver aluminium panels. He produced a high-tech world of steel and sheet metal in the interior and crowned the new extension, to be used as a storage cellar, with a jagged roof. The distorted images of the old sand-stone facades reflected in the mirrored glass of the new buildings have an almost bizarre appearance, especially here in Bordeaux. Even if this seems at first sight to be a mixture of Cru Bordeaux and fast food, Hernandez observed the rules and essential elements of the oenologic production process and designed a perfectly functioning structure.

Bleue est la tendance | Lorsqu'en 1986 le Château d'Arsac a été réouvert, il ne restait du bâtiment d'origine que l'habitation, la cave à fermentation et la remise. Pour être précis, seuls leurs murs ont été conservés. L'architecte Patrick Hernandez a remplacé les anciennes portes en bois par des panneaux brillants en aluminium gris argent. A l'intérieur, il a mis en scène un monde "high tech" en acier et en tôle et il a couronné l'agrandissement abritant le cellier d'un toit cranté. Ici, dans le Bordelais, il est bizarre de voir les façades en calcaire déformées dans les vitrages des nouveaux bâtiments. Même si cela ressemble au premier abord à un mélange de "Cru Bordeaux" et de "fast food", Hernandez a respecté les règles et les composants du processus de production œnologique et conçu une structure parfaitement fonctionnelle. Le bâtiment réservé à l'accueil des visiteurs est particulièrement frappant. C'était à l'époque une nouveauté pour le

Auffällig ist dabei ein Gebäude, das als so-genannter Empfang dient. Damals eine Neu-heit für das Médoc, wo man immer noch zugeknöpft ist und beinahe nur nach Voran-meldung besichtigen kann. Ganz anders die Geste hier: Die schwungvolle Diagonaltei-lung der Giebelfassade in Holz und Glas erinnert an einen zum Empfang geöffneten Vorhang. Innen wird dieser kurvige Diago-nalbalken wieder auftauchen und zum Blick-fang. Außer einem riesigen Kamin für eisige Winterabende geht hier Dekorschmuck gegen Null, allerdings überzeugen Holz oder ein quarzgehärteter und polierter Beton durch ihre präzise Oberflächenqualität. Immer wieder taucht die Leitfarbe Blau auch innen auf – wie im Gärkeller. Den Blick hat der Architekt dabei nicht nur nach vorn, sondern auch nach hinten gewandt: Die blaue Farbe wurde früher als Mittel gegen den Pilzbefall der Mauern benutzt. Besitzer Philippe Raoux gibt gern zu: „Diese Archi-tektursprache hilft mir, meinen Wein besser zu verkaufen."

What stands out is a building serving as a so-called reception. This was, at the time, a novelty for the Médoc where a reserved mentality still prevails and where visits are almost exclusively by appointment only. The gesture here is completely different: the sweeping diagonal division of the glass and wood gabled facade is reminiscent of a set of curtains swept back to receive visitors. Inside, this curved diagonal beam resurfaces and catches the eye. Apart from a huge fire-place for ice-cold winter evenings, there is a complete absence of decoration, though wood or concrete polished and hardened to quartz are convincing in the precise quality of their surfaces. The central colour blue also crops up time and again in the interior – as in the fermentation cellar. The architect hereby turned his gaze not only forwards but also backwards into the past; the colour blue was used in earlier times to prevent fungus attacking the walls. The owner, Philippe Raoux, freely admits that "This architectural language helps me to sell my wine more easily".

Médoc, où on est encore très réservé, et où il est presque obligatoire de prendre rendez-vous pour visiter. Ici, le geste architectural affirme la différence du domaine: la parti-tion diagonale pleine de mouvement du pignon en bois et en verre évoque un rideau ouvert pour accueillir les visiteurs. A l'inté-rieur, l'arc réapparait et devient un élément majeur de la composition. A part une im-mense cheminée pour les glaciales soirées d'hiver, la décoration est pratiquement in-existante; le bois et le béton poli ont en revanche une qualité de surface dont la per-fection impressionne. A l'intérieur, comme dans la cave à fermentation, on retrouve ici et là des taches bleues. En choisissant cette couleur, l'architecte ne s'est pas seulement tourné vers l'avenir, mais aussi vers le passé: le bleu est celui de la „bouillie bordelaise", utilisée pour le sulfatage de la vigne et avec laquelle on désinfectait aussi les murs. Le propriétaire Philippe Raoux le reconnaît volontiers: "Ce langage architectural m'aide à mieux vendre mon vin."

Vorhergehende Seiten:
dynamischer Weiterbau
[1] Empfangsgebäude:
Erinnerung an einen
gerüschten Vorhang
[2] Innen setzt sich der
Schwung des symboli-
schen Vorhangs in der
gekurvten Balkenkon-
struktion fort

Previous pages:
dynamic extension
[1] Reception building:
reminiscent of swept-
back curtains
[2] On the inside the
sweep of the symbolic
curtains is followed
through in the curved
timber-frame structure

Pages précédentes:
prolongation dyna-
mique du bâti
[1] Bâtiment d'accueil:
souvenir d'un rideau
garni de ruches
[2] A l'intérieur, l'élan du
rideau symbolique est
prolongé par des arcs
en bois

[1]

[2]

[3]

[1] Beherrschendes
Accessoire: der Kamin
[2] Zeitgenössisches
Stilmittel: gekonnter
Materialienmix
[3] Sitzmöbel: Nichts
wurde dem Zufall über-
lassen

[1] Dominating accesso-
ry: the fireplace
[2] Contemporary stylis-
tic device: masterly mix
of materials
[3] Seating: nothing was
left to chance

[1] Accessoire dominant:
la cheminée
[2] Eléments contempo-
rains: une mixité des
matériaux très réussie
[3] Sièges: rien n'a été
laissé au hasard

[2]

[1]

[1-2] Degustation: Das Blau der Corporate Identity reicht bis zu den Flaschenetiketten
[3-4] Faßreihen ohne Ende: der Keller von d'Arsac

[1-2] Tasting: the corporate identity blue is even carried though to the labels on the bottles
[3-4] Never-ending rows of barrels: the cellar of d'Arsac

[1-2] Dégustation: le bleu qui identifie l'image de la marque est présent jusque sur les étiquettes
[3-4] Des rangées de tonneaux sans fin: la cave de Château d'Arsac

[3]

[4]

Château
Léoville Poyferré

Farbiges Interieur | Immerhin wird dieses Schloß auf das Jahr 1638 zurückdatiert, und trotz aller Wirren und Schwierigkeiten wird das Château heute noch von den Nachfahren der ursprünglichen Besitzerfamilie gesteuert. Unauffällig integriert sich die Gebäudegruppe ins Weindörfchen St. Julien. Auch hier gilt: Die Überraschung ist innen fällig. Es war der Theaterarchitekt Olivier Brochet, der dort für ausgesprochen gewagte Farbkulissen sorgte. Hier ist der theatralische Effekt wörtlich zunehmen. Farbflächen, Linienführungen, Oberflächen lösen sich auf interessante Weise ab, so daß man vergißt, auf einem Weinbauernhof zu sein!

Colourful interior | This château, at any rate, dates back to the year 1638 and despite all the turmoil and difficulties is still run by the descendants of the original owners. The group of buildings is inconspicuously integrated into the wine village of St. Julien. Here also the interior comes as a surprise. It was the theatre architect, Olivier Brochet, who was responsible for the extremely dramatic, colourful scenery. The theatrical effect is to be taken literally here. Colourful areas, lines, and surfaces alternate in an interesting fashion, making one forget that this is a wine farm!

Un intérieur coloré | Daté de l'an 1638, ce Château, malgré bien des troubles et des difficultés, est toujours dirigé par des descendants des propriétaires d'origine. L'ensemble bâti s'intègre discrètement dans le village viticole de Saint-Julien. Ici aussi, la surprise est à l'intérieur. C'est l'architecte de théâtre Olivier Brochet qui est le maître d'œuvre de ce décor coloré particulièrement osé. Ici, l'effet théâtral est vraiment à prendre au pied de la lettre. Les aplats colorés, les lignes et les surfaces se mêlent d'une manière si intéressante qu'on en oublie presque qu'on se trouve dans une ferme viticole.

[1]

Vorherige Seiten:
Schöne Konfrontation:
Eichenholzfässer und
Glassteinarchitektur
[1-2] Unerwartet: ge-
wagte Farben, strenge
Formen für ein altes
Château

Previous pages: beautiful
confrontation: oak bar-
rels and glass stone
architecture
[1-2] Unexpected: daring
colours and severe forms
for an old château

Pages précédentes: belle
confrontation – ton-
neaux en chêne et ar-
chitecture de pavés de
verre
[1-2] Inattendu: cou-
leurs vives et formes
rigoureuses pour un
vieux château

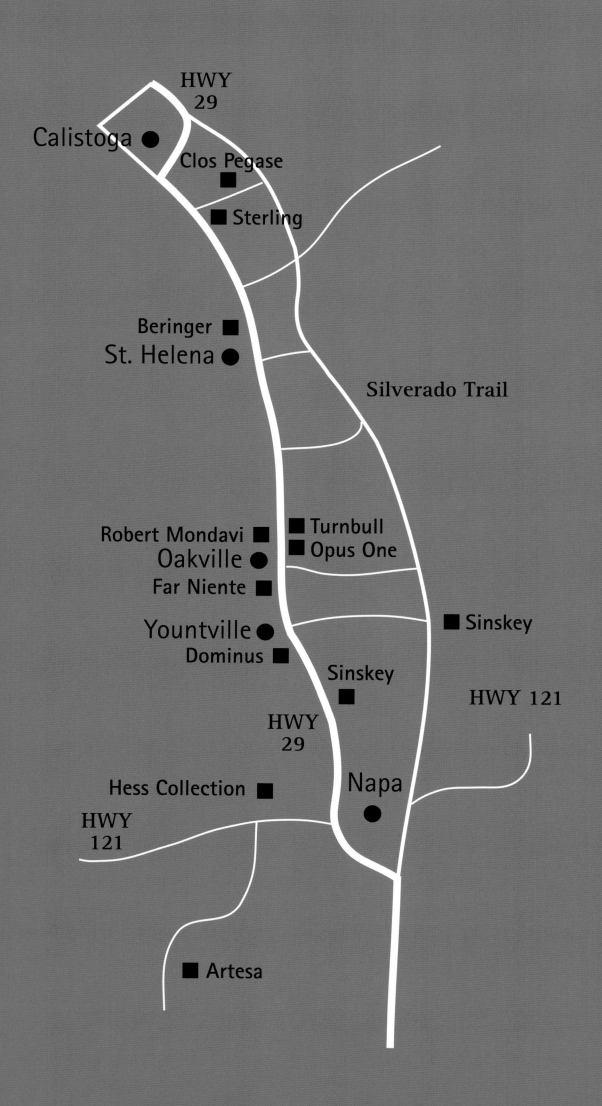

Napa Valley

San Francisco International Airport. Über Down Town, Saussolito, Bay Area nach Nordosten. Irgendwann tauchen dann der kalifornische Highway 29 und das Richtungsschild Napa auf. Aus der Luft betrachtet, wirkt das 50 Kilometer lange Napa Valley wie eine überlange, sanft gebauchte Badewanne, an deren tiefsten Punkt der Napa River fließt. Gewaltige Himmel, tiefes Grün, Sonne, je weiter man nach Norden vordringt, desto wärmer wird es im Sommer; desto kälter im Winter. Über 160 Jahre lang wird hier Wein angebaut: Cabernet Sauvignon, Merlot, Zinvandel. Ein Festival der unterschiedlichen Böden und sich ändernden Klimazonen bringt eine facettenreiche Ernte, hervorragende, fruchtige Weine, deren Stöcke irgendwann einmal den Weg aus Frankreich hierher gefunden haben. Und Weine, die sich deswegen anschicken, ihre Väter im Bordeaux herauszufordern! Ob Napa, Oakville und Yountville im Süden oder St. Helena und Calistoga im Norden – in Napa Valley führen (fast) alle Winzer ein offenes Haus – Besichtigung erwünscht!

San Francisco International Airport. Via Down Town, Saussolito Bay Area to the north east. Somewhere along the way the Californian Highway 29 and the sign for Napa come into view. Seen from above, the 50-km-long Napa Valley takes on the appearance of an over-long, slightly bulbous bathtub with the Napa river flowing along its deepest point. The powerful sky, the dark green and the sun; the further north one advances, the warmer it is in summer and the colder it is in winter. Wine has been grown here for over 160 years: Cabernet Sauvignon, Merlot, Zinfandel. A combination of different soils and changing climatic zones produces a multi-faceted harvest: excellent, fruity wines from vines which at one time or another found their way over here from France. And these wines are now on the point of challenging their forebears in Bordeaux. Be it in Napa, Oakville and Yountville in the south or St. Helena and Calistoga in the north – here in the Napa Valley (almost) all of the wine-growers keep an open house – visitors are always welcome!

Aéroport international de San Francisco. On traverse le centre ville puis le quartier de Saussolito Bay vers le nord-est. Tout à coup, on tombe sur l'autoroute 29 et le panneau Napa. Vu du ciel, Napa valley, une vallée longue de 50 kilomètres, ressemble à une baignoire trop longue et doucement renflée au fond de laquelle coule la rivière Napa. Un ciel violent, un vert profond, le soleil. Plus on remonte vers le nord, plus les étés sont chauds et les hivers froids. Ici, on produit du vin depuis plus de 160 ans: cabernet sauvignon, merlot, zinvandel. Un festival de sols très différents et des zones climatiques variées favorisent des récoltes aux multiples facettes. Les ceps, qui sont un jour venus de France, donnent des vins fruités exceptionnels qui se préparent à lancer un défi à leurs ancêtres du Bordelais. Que ce soit à Napa, à Oakville et Yountville au sud, ou encore à Helena et Calistoga au nord, presque tous les vignerons de Napa valley ouvrent leurs portes. Les visiteurs sont les bienvenus!

Beringer Vineyards

ringer

Architektur mit Schiebung | Es ist wohl die älteste Napa Winery, die ununterbrochen (auch zu Zeiten der Prohibition) bewirtschaftet wurde; ein Hort der Tradition und Geschichte. So steht dann diese Gründung der deutschen Brüder Jacob und Frederik Beringer (1876) heute nicht für ein modernes Architekturbeispiel, sondern für ein stolzes altes Weinschlößchen, wo sich europäische und amerikanische Bautraditionen früherer Jahrhunderte treffen. Der Weinkeller aus den Gründerjahren von Beringer erinnert an die trutzige Haltung eines militärischen Forts aus den amerikanischen Bürgerkriegen. Das eigentliche architektonische Juwel ist das sogenannte „Rhine House" (erbaut 1884 für Frederik). Der kalifornische Architekt Schroepfer kopierte einfach das deutsche Domizil der Beringer-

Architecture shifted | It is the oldest Napa winery to have been managed continuously (even during the Prohibition); a hoard of tradition and history. Founded by the German brothers, Jakob and Frederik Beringer (1876), this winery is therefore not representative, today, of modern architecture, but rather of an impressive, old wine chateau where European and American architectural traditions from earlier centuries meet. The wine cellar from the time Beringer was founded is reminiscent of the defiant stance of a military fort in the American civil wars. The real architectonic jewel is the so-called "Rhine House" (built in 1884 for Frederik). The Californian architect, Schroepfer, simply copied the Beringer

Une architecture "déplacée" | Beringer, le plus ancien domaine de Napa, exploité sans interruption même pendant la Prohibition, est un lieu de tradition et d'histoire. Créé par les frères allemands Jakob et Frederik Beringer en 1876, il ne compte pas aujourd'hui parmi les exemples de l'architecture moderne. C'est un manoir du vin, vieux et fier, où les traditions constructives européennes et américaines des siècles passés se sont rencontrées. Le chai, qui date de la création, rappelle l'attitude résistante d'un fort militaire de la guerre de sécession. Le véritable joyau architectural est la "Rhine House", construite en 1884 pour Frederik. L'architecte californien A. Schroepfer a tout simplement copié le domicile allemand de la famille Beringer, mais il a employé

[1]

Familie, verwendete allerdings kalifornische Redwood-Hölzer und behauenen Kalkstein aus der Gegend. Das mächtige Dach mit den erhabenen Türmchen weist das Haus fast als einen Anrainer wilhelminischer Vororte Berlins aus, die wiederum oft mittelalterliche Motive aufnahmen. Längst ist das „Rhine House" kein Wohnhaus mehr, sondern öffentlich für den Shop und die Bar zugänglich. Viele kleine Interieur-Kostbarkeiten sind erhalten. So auch die bunten Glasfenster, deren Motivik plastisch auf den früheren Zweck des jeweiligen Raumes hinweisen. Helle deutsche Eiche wurde für Treppen oder Vertäfelungen verwendet und im kräftigen belgischen Stil des Art Nouveau verziert. Eine Schmunzette am Rande: das ältere „Hudson House", wo Bruder Jacob residierte, mußte für den Neubau des „Rhine House" um 200 Fuß verschoben werden. Beringer ist also ein Architekturdenkmal mit Schiebung.

family's German domicile, albeit using local Californian redwood timber and limestone. The house with its immense roof and lofty turrets could almost be identified as belonging to the Wilhelminian suburbs of Berlin, though on the other hand also takes up a medieval motif. The "Rhine House" has not been lived in for a long time; it is now accessible to the public as an entrance to the shop and bar. Numerous small treasures in the interior have been preserved, as have the colourful glass windows whose motif is concrete evidence of the earlier use of the respective rooms. Light German oak was used for stairs and panelling and decorated in a rich Belgian Art Nouveau style. An anecdote around the edge: the former "Hudson House" where brother Jakob resided, had to be moved 200 feet to build the "Rhine House". Beringer is, therefore, a "shifted" memorial to architecture.

du séquoia californien et du calcaire de la région. Le toit imposant, d'où émergent de petites tours, pourrait faire croire que la maison se trouve dans une des banlieues de Berlin construites sous l'empereur Guillaume, à l'époque où l'on s'inspirait beaucoup de motifs moyenâgeux. Il y a longtemps que la "Rhine House" n'est plus un bâtiment d'habitation, mais un lieu ouvert au public, avec boutique et bar. A l'intérieur, plusieurs objets précieux ont été conservés, comme les vitraux colorés, dont le motif symbolise l'ancienne utilisation de chaque pièce. Escaliers et boiseries en chêne clair importé d'Allemagne sont décorés dans le style vigoureux de l'Art Nouveau belge. Une anecdote en passant: l'ancienne "Hudson House", où résidait Jakob, le frère de Frederik, a dû être déplacée de 70 métres pour permettre la construction de la "Rhine house". Beringer est donc un monument d'architecture "déplacé".

Vorherige Seiten links oben: Rhine House; rechts: Weinkeller
[1] Glasmalereien prägen das Interieur: Glasdetail innen: B steht hier für Beringer
[2] „Founders Room": eine Bar mit artifiziellen Holzschnitzereien im heutigen Schank- und Probierraum

Previous pages, top left: the Rhine House; right: wine cellar
[1] Stained glass dominates the interior: glass detail on the inside: B stands for Beringer
[2] "Founders room": a bar with artificial wooden carvings in the serving and tasting area

Pages précédentes, à gauche, en haut: la "Rhine house"; à droite: la cave à vin
[1] L'ambiance intérieure est dominée par les vitraux colorés ; le B est l'insigne de la famille Beringer
[2] "La salle des fondateurs", un bar avec des sculptures sur bois, est devenue salon de dégustation

Robert Mondavi

Kalifornische Grandezza | Ein weitge-
spanntes Bogenhaus breitet sich im Schutze
eines schlanken Turmes aus. Kein anderes
Motiv als das Eingangsgebäude von Robert
Mondavi hat sich so eindeutig als optisches
Symbol für den Weinbau im Napa Valley
durchgesetzt. Es schmückt die Weinetiketten
in den besten Restaurants und Hotels.
Mondavis steinernes Weingut ist ein höchst
eleganter Vertreter eines Baustils aus dem
16. Jahrhundert, der für Erfolg und Tradition
der spanischen Missionare-Patres steht.
Selbstverständlich ist dieses Ensemble büh-
nenreif arrangiert so, daß es vom Highway
aus gut sichtbar ist und als Tor und Eintritt
zu einer fremden Welt begriffen wird: Hier
hält eine Winzerdynastie neuen Stils Hof!
Das Ensemble ist konsequent, den Funktio-
nen folgend, zweigeteilt. Erstens: Ganz dem

Californian grandeur | A wide-spanned
arc-shaped house spreads out under the
shelter of a slender tower. No other motif
than the entrance building by Robert
Mondavi has been so explicitly successful in
becoming an optical symbol of wine-growing in the Napa Valley, since it is pictured on
the wine labels in the best restaurants and
hotels. Mondavi's stone estate is an extrem-
ely elegant example of an architectural style
from the 16th century, standing for the success and tradition of the Spanish Missionary
Fathers. Naturally, this ensemble is arranged,
as if on a stage, in such as way that it is
clearly visible from the highway and is also
seen as the gateway and entrance to a foreign world: a new-style wine-growers'
dynasty holds court here! The ensemble is
separated, in a logically consistent manner,
into two halves, according to the functions
of each. Firstly, due entirely to the sunny climate, the southern parts of the building

La grandeur californienne | Un bâtiment
en forme d'arc largement tendu s'étale sous
la protection d'une tour élancée. Aucun
autre motif n'a réussi à s'imposer de manière aussi significative comme symbole des
vignobles de Napa valley que celui de ce
domaine qui orne les étiquettes des vins
servis dans les meilleurs hôtels et restaurants. Réalisé en pierre, Mondavi est un
exemple particulièrement élégant du style
de construction du 16ème siècle, symbole
du succès et de la tradition des mission-
naires espagnols. Evidemment, cet ensemble
est mis en scène afin d'être bien visible de
l'autoroute et immédiatement perçu comme
un portail marquant l'accès à un monde
exceptionnel. Ici, une dynastie de vignerons
tient une cour d'un nouveau style! Pour
répondre aux différentes fonctions, l'ensemble est décomposé de manière rigoureu-
se en deux parties. A cause du climat très
ensoleillé, la partie sud du bâtiment forme

sonnigen Klima geschuldet, bilden die südlichen Bauteile in einer symbolischen V-Form (für Victory) einen schattigen Schutzwall um Höfe und eine kleine Festwiese für Sommerfeste – die Weinstöcke in Greifnähe. Weit überragende Dächer, rustikales Mauerwerk und tiefe schattige Säulengänge sind die Requisiten für gelungene Feste. Lobby, Show- und die Tasting Rooms, würden mit ihrem gediegenen Interieur so manchem First Class Hotel gut zu Gesicht stehen. Nördlich schließen dann die „Fabrikteile" an: Große Hallen, die aber zum publikumsöffentlichen Teil hinter prächtigen Mauern verborgen bleiben. DieGesamtbotschaft: Südliche Grandezza, erdverbunden, traditionell und unnachahmbar – ein schönes Stück Kalifornien!

form a shady protective wall, in a symbolic V-shape (for victory), around courtyards and a small festival ground used for summer fairs – the vines within reach. Considerably overhanging roofs, rustic masonry and low, shady colonnades are the requisites for successful fairs. The lobby, show and tasting rooms with their fine interiors would become any first class hotel. The northern half houses the "factory parts": large halls, which however remain hidden behind magnificent walls in the area open to the public. The overall message conveyed is one of southern grandeur, an air of earthiness, tradition and a style impossible to imitate - a wonderful piece of California!

un mur protecteur disposé symboliquement en forme de "V" (pour victoire) et abritant des cours et une petite prairie à proximité des vignes pour les garden-parties. Des toits aux larges débords, une maçonnerie rustique et de profondes colonnades ombragées sont les accessoires indispensables à des fêtes réussies. L'aménagement intérieur du vestibule, des espaces d'exposition et des salons de dégustation pourrait concurrencer celui de certains hôtels de luxe. Au nord, se trouve "l'usine": de grandes halles de production, dissimulées derrière des murs magnifiques dans la partie ouverte au public. Le message est clair: ici, règne la grandeur du sud, attachée à la terre, traditionnelle et inimitable. Un beau morceau de Californie!

[1]

[2]

[3]

[1] Folklore: Wandleuch-
te im Säulengang
[2-3] Turm und Torge-
bäude wurden zum
Markenzeichen von
Mondavi: die Gebäude
umschließen V-förmig
einen großen Patio
Nachfolgende Seiten:
Weinprobe mit Weinber-
gen fast zum Anfassen

[1] Folklore: wall-light in
the columned corridor
[2-3] The tower and
gateway have become
trademarks of Mondavi:
the buildings surround a
large patio in a V-shape
Following pages: wine
tasting: with vineyards
almost close enough to
touch

[1] Folklorique: les
appliques murales dans
la colonnade
[2-3] Tour et portail
sont devenus les
insignes de Mondavi ;
les bâtiments entourant
le grand patio forment
le V de la victoire
Pages suivantes: dégus-
tation – si proche des
vignes que l'on pourrait
presque les toucher

Robert Mondavi

„In den frühen 60er Jahren war ich als Mitglied des Wein-Institutes mit einer Gruppe in den Menlo Park eingeladen, um die neue Hauptverwaltung der Zeitschrift Sunset zu besichtigen. Als ich dieses wunderschöne Gebäude sah, dachte ich mir: Wenn ich je ein Weingut baue, dann soll es so aussehen. Es hat diese warme Ausstrahlung. Ich rief also Bill Lane an, den Inhaber von Sunset, und fragte ihn, wer dieses Gebäude entworfen hatte. Er sagte mir, daß es gar kein Architekt, sondern ein renommierter Designer namens Cliff May gewesen war."

„...Das Weingut, das Cliff dann (für Mondavi, Anm. d.Red.) entwarf, war eines im californischen Missions-Stil, mit Anlehnungen an alte spanische Klöster und Haciendas. Cliffs Entwurf strahlte Eleganz und Schlichtheit aus: Die Struktur leicht und luftig in der Anmutung, keineswegs monumental oder industriell im Aussehen; das niedrige V-förmige Gebäude mit weitgeöffnetem Bogengang in der Mitte und zwei öffnenden Armen an den Seiten, die sozusagen die Weinberge umarmen. Die Spitze des V zeigt auf den Highway, und direkt im anmutigen Bogengang hat Cliff ... - wenn man von außen hineinsieht - einen wunderschönen Turm plaziert, ein Glockenturm in der Art wie jene, die man neben mittelalterlichen Kirchen in Italien sieht. "

Auszüge aus HARVEST OF JOY, MY PASSION, MY LIFE, copyright © 1998 von Robert Mondavi, abgedruckt mit freundlicher Genehmigung von Harcourt, Inc., Orlando, USA

"In the early 1960s, as a member of Wine Institute, I had been among a group invited to Menlo Park to see the new headquaters of Sunset magazine. When I saw that beautiful building, I said, 'By gosh, if I ever build a winery, this is what I want! It has that warm feel.' So I called Bill Lane, the owner of Sunset magazine, and asked him who had actually designed Sunset House. He told me it was not an architect, but a highly respected designer named Cliff May."

"...The winery Cliff envisioned (for Mondavi, Editor's note) was a rendition of the California mission style, with flavours of old Spanish monasteries and haciendas. The design exuded elegance and simplicity. The structure was light and airy in feel, by no means monumental in scale or industrial in look. The low, V-shaped building had a broad, open archway in the middle and two arms opening out to embrace the vineyards behind. The point of the V faced the highway, and through the graceful archway, as you faced the winery, ... Cliff had placed a lovely campanile, a bell tower like the ones you see beside medieval churches in Italy."

Excerpts from HARVEST OF JOY, MY PASSION, MY LIFE, copyright © 1998 by Robert Mondavi, reprinted permission of Harcourt, Inc., Orlando, USA

"Au début des années 60, en tant que membre de l'Institut du vin, j'ai fait partie d'un groupe invité au Menlo Park pour visiter le nouveau bâtiment de l'administration centrale du magazine 'Sunset'. Lorsque j'ai vu cette magnifique réalisation, j'ai pensé: Si tu as un jour l'occasion de construire un domaine viticole, il devra ressembler à ce bâtiment, avoir ce rayonnement chaleureux. J'ai aussitôt appelé Bill Lane, le propriétaire de 'Sunset', et je lui ai demandé qui avait conçu L'immeuble. Il m'a répondu que ce n'était pas un architecte mais un designer renommé du nom de Cliff May."

" ... Le domaine que Cliff a ensuite conçu (pour Mondavi, note de l'auteur) était dans le style des missions californiennes, inspiré des anciens monastères espagnols et des haciendas. Le projet de Cliff rayonnait d'élégance et de pureté: la structure Légère, aérienne et pleine de charme n'a une apparence ni monumentale, ni industrielle; le bâtiment bas en forme de V a des galeries à arcades largement ouvertes au centre et deux bras tendus sur les côtés, comme pour embrasser les vignes. La pointe du V ouvertes au centre et deux bras tendus sur les côtés, comme pour embrasser les vignes. La pointe du V désigne l'autoroute et Cliff a placé directement dans la charmante galerie à arcades une magnifique tour, un campanile dans le style de ceux que l'on voit à côté des églises italiennes moyenâgeuses."

Extraits de HARVEST OF JOY, MY PASSION, MY LIFE, copyright © 1998 par Robert Mondavi, reproduits avec l'aimable autorisation de Harcourt, Inc. Orlando, USA

Trefethen Vineyards

fethen

The prototype | An intense pink, sometimes also cerise or violet – depending on the moods of the North Californian sun in the changing seasons – compels the drivers on Highway 29, between Napa and Oakville shortly after Oak Knoll Avenue, to look to the east. A classical farmhouse with a proud gable - the prototype, if you like, of a Californian wine farm. This estate, more than 100 years old, was built for the Eshcol family in 1886 by the architect, Captain Hamden McIntyre, said to be the leading wine-grower of this period. Today Trefethen is one of the few estates to have survived undamaged and practically unchanged. Naturally it is classified as an historical building. In former times, a horse-driven lift or hoist would make sure that the grapes from the harvest reached the highest of the three floors, from where they were thrown into the presses.

Der Prototyp | Ein kräftiges Rosarot, manchmal auch Pink oder Violett – das ist abhängig von den Launen der nordkalifornischen Sonne in den wechselhaften Jahreszeiten – zwingt die Blicke des Autofahrers auf dem Highway 29 zwischen Napa und Oakville kurz hinter der Oak Knoll Avenue nach Osten. Ein klassisches Farmhaus mit stolzem Giebel; wenn man so will, der Prototyp eines kalifornischen Weinbauernhofes. Über 100 Jahre alt, 1886 für die Familie Eshcol gebaut vom Architekten Captain Hamden McIntyre, dem man nachsagt, er sei der führende Weinbaumeister jener Jahre gewesen. Heute ist Trefethen eines der wenigen Weingüter, das unbeschadet und so gut wie unverändert die Zeiten überstanden hat. Selbstverständlich steht es unter Denkmalschutz. Ein durch Pferde angetriebener Aufzug sorgte früher dafür, daß die Trauben in der Ernte ins obere der drei Geschosse gelangte, um von dort in die Pressen geworfen zu werden.

Le prototype | Un rouge vif, parfois aussi du rose ou du violet – selon l'humeur du soleil de la Californie du nord au rythme de saisons capricieuses – attire les regards des automobilistes roulant vers l'est sur l'autoroute 29 entre Napa et Oakville, juste derrière l'avenue Oak Knoll. Une ferme classique avec un fier pignon , un peu comme le prototype d'une ferme viticole américaine. Vieille de plus d'un siècle, elle a été construite pour la famille Eshcol par le capitaine Hamden McIntyre, architecte, dont on dit qu'il aurait été le maître d'œuvre des vignerons de l'époque. Autrefois, c'était grâce à un ascenseur actionné par un cheval que le raisin de la récolte arrivait au dernier des trois étages avant d'être jeté dans le pressoir.

Das Haus ist in den siebziger Jahren renoviert worden, und durch Eugene Trefethen wurde eine neue Phase des Weinbaus eingeleitet. Im engen Napa Tal wechseln die Qualitäten der Böden und die klimatischen Voraussetzungen rasch und unverhofft. Hier sind die Voraussetzungen für Chardonnay gut – Trefethen produziert einen entsprechend hochdekorierten Weißwein. Ebenso klassisch ist die Baukunst: ein hallenartiges Farmhaus unter flach abgeschlepptem Satteldach mit den obligatorischen Lüftungstürmchen am First, symbolisch überhöht durch die optimistische altrosafarbene Holzfront – Zeichen für Hoffnung auf Zukunft im Napa Valley.

The house was renovated in the seventies and a new phase of wine-growing was introduced by Eugene Trefethen. In the narrow Napa Valley the soil quality and the climatic conditions change rapidly and unexpectedly. The conditions are good here for Chardonnay – Trefethen produces an accordingly highly decorative white wine. Equally classical is the architecture: a hall-like farmhouse beneath a flattened saddle roof with the obligatory ventilation turrets on its ridge: symbolically heightened by the optimistic old-rose-coloured wooden front – a sign of the hope of a future in the Napa Valley.

Trefethen est un des rares domaines viticoles qui soit sorti indemne d'une période difficile, et il est bien sûr considéré comme un monument historique. La maison a été rénovée dans les années 70 et elle est entrée, grâce à Eugene E. Trefethen, dans une nouvelle phase de la culture du vin. Dans l'étroite vallée de la Napa, la qualité des sols et les conditions climatiques se transforment rapidement et à l'improviste. Là, les conditions sont idéales pour le chardonnay et Trefethen produit donc un vin blanc "très décoré". L'architecture est classique: une ferme en forme de halle sous un toit à deux pentes, avec les tours de ventilation obligatoires sur le faîtage. La façade en bois du bâtiment a été symboliquement soulignée par une peinture vieux rose, emblème de l'espoir que Napa valley place dans l'avenir.

[1]

Vorherige Seiten:
Kontinuität – neue und
historische Ansichten
[1] Chamäleon: Das
Gebäude wechselt seine
Farbe – wie es die
Sonne befiehlt

Previous pages:
continuity – new and
historical views
[1] Chameleon: the build-
ing changes colour – at
the sun's command

Pages précédentes :
continuité – façade his-
torique, nouvelle façade
[1] Caméléon: le bâti-
ment change de couleur
selon les caprices du
soleil

Sterling Vineyards

Das Weinmuseum | Weiß und kristallin blitzen die einzelnen Bauteile des Weinguts durch das Grün der Nadelbäume. Ein kühnes Ensemble, oben auf einem Hügel, südlich von Calistoga, so wie es die großen Architekten Le Corbusier oder José Luis Sert mit der Kapelle in Ronchamp und anderen Bauten einer muralen Architektur der Kykladen abgeschaut haben könnten. Die Sterling Vineyards, die 1964 von Peter Newton gegründet und 1983 in den Seagram Konzern integriert wurden, bieten ein Procedere dazu an, wie es erst kürzlich im größeren Maßstab im „Getty Center" bei Santa Monica (L. A.) zelebriert wurde: kein individueller Zugang, sondern eine „tram", hier in Form eines alpinen Sesselliftes, der im großen Schwung über einen Seerosenteich und den hellgrünen Hügelsockel die Besucher einschweben läßt.

The wine museum | The individual parts of the estate gleam white and crystalline through the green of the conifers. A bold ensemble, up on a hill, south of Calistoga, evocative of the great architects Le Corbusier or José Luis Sert with the chapel in Ronchamp and other buildings, based on an architecture that could have pinched from the Cyclades. The Sterling Vineyards, founded in 1964 by Peter Newton and integrated into the Seagram concern in 1983, offer a procedure as was only recently celebrated, on a larger scale, in the "Getty Center" in Santa Monica (L. A.): no individual access, rather a "tram", here in the form of an alpine chair-lift, allowing visitors to glide in one sweep above a water-lily pond and the pale green base of the hill.

Le Musée du vin | Blancs et cristallins, les différents bâtiments de ce domaine brillent à travers les verts sapins. Cet ensemble audacieux, posé au sommet d'une colline au sud de Calistoga, évoque la chapelle de Ronchamp de Le Corbusier ou les œuvres de José Luis Sert et d'autres grands concepteurs inspirés par l'architecture minérale des Cyclades. Fondé en 1964 par Peter Newton et intégré en 1983 dans le groupe industriel Seagram, Sterling Vineyards offre une visite dont l'échelle vient seulement d'être dépassée depuis peu par le "Getty Center" de Santa Monica, près de Los Angeles. Pas d'accès individuel, mais un télésiège qui fait flotter les visiteurs au dessus de prairies vert tendre et d'un étang couvert de nénuphars.

On arrival at the chair-lift station the visitors are confronted with an estate divided into two halves. The visitors' centre, which is being newly renovated for the start of the new millennium, is situated at the top of the hill. To the south of the main track the "wine farm (itself) can be viewed, the walk through it ending on a magnificent roof terrace". The wine-making process is laid open; visitors can walk through the various stages in a self-guided tour. Peter Newton created the first "wine museum" in the world. Just like in a Greek village one passes narrow alleyways and steep steps; just like in Greece there are hatches and embrasures to keep the sun out instead of windows, despite being in the north (of California).

A l'arrivée à la "station de montagne" du téléphérique, les installations sont réparties sur deux zones: au sommet, le centre d'accueil pour les visiteurs, restauré à l'occasion du passage au 21ème siècle; au sud du chemin principal, la ferme viticole proprement dite, dont la visite s'achève sur une magnifique terrasse. Le processus de vinification est dévoilé au public et chacun peut le découvrir à son rythme au cours d'une visite non guidée. Peter Newton a ainsi créé le premier musée des vins du monde. Comme dans un village grec, on se glisse le long d'étroites venelles et d'escaliers ; comme en Grèce, et bien que l'on soit au nord (de la Californie !), les baies sont remplacées par de petites fenêtres en forme de meurtrières.

[1]

An der Bergstation des Sesselliftes angekommen, präsentiert sich eine zweigeteilte Anlage. Oben auf dem Hügel liegt das Besucherzentrum, das zur Jahrtausendwende frisch restauriert wird. Südlich des Hauptweges ist der eigentliche „Weinbauernhof" zu besichtigen, dessen Begehung auf einer prächtigen Dachterrasse endet. Der Prozeß des Weinmachens wird offen gelegt, kann von den Besuchern in einer Self Guided Tour erlaufen werden. Peter Newton hat das erste „Museum des Weins" auf der Welt geschaffen. Wie in einem griechischen Dorf passiert man schmale Gassenschluchten und steile Treppen, wie in Griechenland gibt es statt Fenster sonnenabwehrende Luken und Scharten, obwohl man im Norden (von Kalifornien) ist.

[1] Einheitlich: Die murale und weiße Architektur beginnt mit dem Portal an der Zufahrtsstraße
[2] Mediterran: Der Eindruck eines kykladischen Dorfes wird vor allem durch offene Glockentürme hervorgerufen

[1] Uniform: the white architecture begins with the portal on the access road
[2] Mediterranean: an impression of a Cycladic village is especially created by the open bell towers

[1] Unité: l'architecture blanche et minérale commence avec le portail d'entrée donnant sur la route d'accès
[2] Méditerranéen: ce sont avant tout les clochers qui font penser à un village des Cyclades

[1]

[1] Dachterrasse: der „schönste" Blick ins Napa Valley
[2] Mitten im „Dorf": Tonnendächer mit Durchblick
[3] Gut getarnt: Die großen Baumassen einer Weinfabrik verschwinden hinter dörflichen Mauern

[1] Roof terrace: the "most beautiful" view over the Napa Valley
[2] "Village" centre: view through the barrel roofs
[3] Well camouflaged: the great mass of buildings of a wine factory disappear behind village walls

[1] Toit terrasse: la "plus belle vue" sur la Napa valley
[2] Au milieu du village: les toitures voûtées en berceau autorisent des échappées
[3] Bien camouflé: l'importante masse construite d'une "fabrique à vin" disparaît derrière des murs de village

[2]

[3]

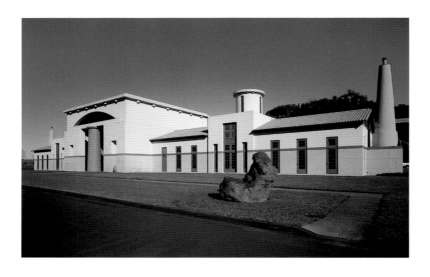

Clos Pegase

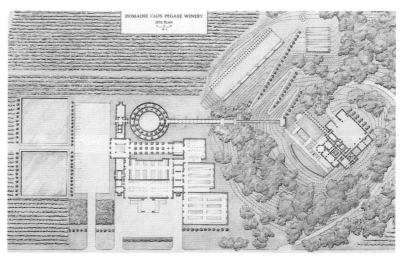

[1]

Fabelwesen | Michael Graves, einer der Hausarchitekten des Disney-Konzerns, ist bekanntermaßen ein eigenwilliger Baumeister. Er hatte 1984 einen stark besetzten Wettbewerb für den Bau von Clos Pegase in der Hochphase der Postmoderne gewonnen. Heute zeigt sich aber, daß dieses erdfarbene, mit kräftigen Farbakzenten versehene „Fabelwesen aus Stein und Putz" alle kritischen Zeitgeister überlebt hat: Es ist ein Bauwerk von klassischer Qualität, ein Ort um Wein reifen zu lassen, aber vor allem auch ein Platz der Muse und der Kunst. Graves hat in seiner symmetrisch bestimmten Anlage die Spiegelachse zur imaginären Trennungslinie zwischen Arbeit und Spaß gemacht.

Mythical creature | Michael Graves, one of the Disney concern's in-house architects, is known to be an unconventional architect. In 1984 he won a very well represented competition to build the Clos Pegase in the golden age of postmodernism. Today, however, it turns out that this earth-coloured "mythical creature of stone and plaster", strongly accentuated with colour, has survived all the critical climates of opinion. It is a building with a classic quality, a place to let wine mature, but also, above all, a place of leisure and art. In his symmetrically designed estate, Graves turned the axis of symmetry into an imaginary dividing line between work and play.

Créature de contes | Tout le monde sait que Michael Graves, un des architectes du groupe Disney, est un maître d'œuvre volontariste. En 1984, aux heures de gloire du Postmodernisme, il a gagné le concours très bien fréquenté lancé pour la réalisation du Clos Pegase. On s'aperçoit aujourd'hui que cette "créature de contes en pierre et en plâtre", dont les tons de terre alternent avec quelques accents de couleur, a survécu aux effets de mode. C'est une œuvre d'une qualité classique, un lieu destiné au mûrissement du vin et avant tout un endroit consacré à l'art et aux loisirs.

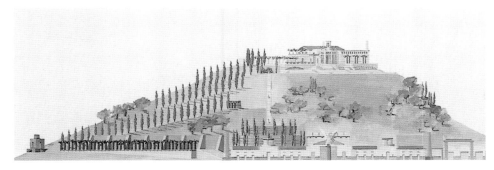

[2]

[1] Übersichtsplan des Architekten Michael Graves: links Weingut, rechts Privathaus
[2] Gezeichnete Ansicht des Architekten Michael Graves: Auf der Hügelkrone liegt das Privathaus des Winzers

[1] Outline plan by the architect, Michael Graves: left vineyard, right private residence
[2] View as drawn by the architect, Michael Graves: the wine-grower's private residence is situated on top of the hill

[1] Plan d'ensemble de l'architecte Michael Graves: à gauche, le domaine ; à droite, la maison d'habitation
[2] Façade dessinée par l'architecte Michael Graves: au sommet de la colline, la maison du vigneron

[1]

[2]

[3]

[4]

[2] Ausschnitt:
Eingangsfront mit Kamin
(Büro des Winzers)
[3] Schöner Rücken:
„Fabrik"hallen für Wein-
verarbeitung und Lage-
rung
[4] Südansicht mit An-
lieferung und Expedition
(Architektenzeichnung)

[2] Detail: frontage of the
entrance building with
chimney (wine grower's
office)
[3] Lovely rear: "factory"
halls for wine processing
and storage
[4] South view with
delivery and expedition
(architect's drawing)

[2] Fragment: façade
d'entrée avec cheminée
– le bureau du vigneron
[3] Un "joli dos": les
halles de "l'usine" de
production du vin et les
entrepôts
[4] Façade sud avec
livraison et expédition
(dessin de l'architecte)

Wir Flaneure bestaunen ein janusköpfiges Gebilde, das sich jeweils links und rechts einer gewaltigen Säule, die im Zentrum steht, entwickelt. Aber es sind zwei unterschiedliche Dinge im Spiel: Ratio und Emotio, Stand- und Spielbein. Rechts der unsichtbaren Trennlinie wird gearbeitet und verwaltet. Die entsprechende Südansicht, wo die Expedition abgewickelt wird, hat Michael Graves wie ein Altarbild aufgefaltet und zur Huldigung eines ländlichen Industriebetriebes werden lassen, denn alles wirkt wie eine aufgeräumte Ziegelei außer Diensten. Meistens bewachen die Kamine rauchlos die Anlage wie Castor und Pollux.

Strolling along we marvel at a Janus-faced creation both to the right and left of a colossal pillar in the centre. But there are two different factors at play; reason and emotion, the standing leg and free leg. The work and administration are carried out to the right of the imaginary dividing line. The corresponding south view, the location for the expedition, was unfolded like an altarpiece by Michael Graves and turned into an homage to a rural industrial firm; the overall effect produced is one of a cleaned-up, out-of-service brickworks. The smokeless chimneys, which in actual fact are useless, watch over the estate like Castor and Pollux.

Graves a basé sa composition symétriquement ordonnée sur un axe symbolisant la ligne de démarcation entre travail et plaisir. Nous, les flâneurs, nous regardons avec étonnement les deux visages de Janus, disposés à gauche et à droite d'une énorme colonne plantée au centre du complexe. Il y a deux réalités en jeu: le rationnel et l'émotionnel; la jambe qui porte et la jambe qui joue. A droite de la ligne imaginaire, on travaille et on administre. Michael Graves a développé la façade sud, derrière laquelle on prépare les expéditions, comme l'image d'un autel déplié. Il en a fait un hommage à une industrie provinciale: l'ensemble ressemble à

Links liegen die Caves, die geheimnisvoll illuminierten Kellergänge, wo regelmäßig intime Konzerte und Lesungen stattfinden und ganz nebenbei, so scheint es, lagert und reift dort ein Wein, der als einer der besten im Tal gilt. Links liegt auch die Bar, links hängen wunderschöne Gemälde aus der Sammlung Shrems. Links steht eine italienische Bacchus-Figur, links entstand ein Skulpturengarten, bespickt mit einer Fingerkuppe des Künstlers César. Schaut man hinauf auf den dahinter liegenden Hügel, thront links aus der Achse verschoben, die imposante Residenz des Winzers, auch sie ist ein Entwurf von Michael Graves.

To the right are the "caves", the mysteriously illuminated cellar arcades where intimate concerts and readings regularly take place and where, seemingly quite incidentally, a wine is stored and matured that is considered the best in the valley. The bar is situated to the left; wonderful paintings from the Shrems collection are hung on the left side. Also on the left is an Italian Bacchus figure; a sculpture garden was created on the left, with a fingertip of the artist, César. If we look up to the hill behind this garden, we can see the wine-grower's imposing residence standing in solitary splendour, shifted to the left of the axis; this too is one of Michael Graves' designs.

une tuilerie hors service. Des cheminées, qui sont en réalité sans fonction, aucune fumée ne s'échappe jamais. Telles Castor et Pollux, elles montent la garde devant les installations. A gauche se trouvent les "Caves", des celliers mystérieusement illuminés où se tiennent régulièrement des concerts et des conférences intimistes et où, presque secondairement, repose et mûrit un vin qui passe pour un des meilleurs de cette vallée. A gauche, il y a aussi le "Bar", avec de superbes toiles appartenant à la collection Shrems et un portrait de Bacchus qui vient d'Italie. Toujours à gauche, on a créé un jardin de sculptures dans lequel se trouve l'empreinte du pouce de l'artiste français César.

[1]

Vorherige Seiten: Parade der Tanks – Michael Graves überläßt bei der Gestaltung nichts dem Zufall, auch nicht im Cuvier
[1-2] folgende Seiten: Kulturpalast – Impressionen aus den Kellertunneln, die unter anderem als Museum, Showroom und Veranstaltungsraum dienen

Previous pages: parade of tanks – Michael Graves leaves nothing to chance in his design, not even in the cuvier
[1-2] Following pages: cultural palace – impressions from the cellar tunnels which serve, amongst other things, as a museum, showroom and performance area

Pages précédentes: parade de citernes – Michael Graves ne laisse rien au hasard, pas même dans le cuvier
[1-2] et pages suivantes: palais de la culture – quelques ambiances dans les caves roûtées qui servent entre autres de musée, d'espace d'exposition et de salle de spectacle

[2]

[2]

Dieser überläßt unten in der Winery auch innen nichts dem Zufall, leistet sich keine Unachtsamkeit, sondern gestaltet auch die Produktions- und Bürobereiche räumlich und plastisch mit demselben Aufwand und Überraschungseffekt – sichtbar in der sechs Meter hohen Vorhalle zum Chefbüro, die mit einer runden Lichtkuppel gekrönt wird.

Clos Pegase könnte zu den Meisterwerken einer postmodernen Architekturauffassung gezählt werden. Könnte. Es ist heute eher ein Kunst-Bauwerk klassi(zisti)scher Aura. Ohne wirkliche stilistische Einordnung. Geadelt durch hohe Besucherzahlen und eine exzellente Weinqualität.

Below in the winery, in the interior also, he leaves nothing to chance and allows no carelessness; instead he also designs the production and office areas, spatially and vividly, with the same extravagance and surprise effect – visible in the 6-meter-high entrance hall of the executive office, surmounted with a round light cupola.

Clos Pegase "could" be counted among the masterpieces of a post-modern architectural conception. I say could because today it is more of an architectural work of art with a classic(al) aura. Not really belonging to any one stylistic category. Ennobled due to its high number of visitors and the excellent quality of its wine.

Si l'on regarde en haut vers la colline située derrière le domaine, on voit trôner, légèrement désaxé vers la gauche, l'imposante résidence du vigneron, une autre œuvre de Michael Graves. Même en bas, dans "l'usine" à vin, l'architecte n'a rien laissé au hasard. Ne s'autorisant aucune inattention, il a conçu les départements de production fonctionnellement et plastiquement avec le même soin et les mêmes effets de surprise, particulièrement visibles dans le hall de réception du bureau du directeur, couronné par une coupole vitrée circulaire, posée à six mètres de haut.

Le Clos Pegase aurait pu compter parmi les ouvrages majeurs du visionnaire postmoderne de l'architecture. Aurait pu! C'est devenu plutôt un ouvrage à l'aura classique auquel il est difficile d'attribuer une classification stylistique, et qui est anobli par le nombre très élevé des visiteurs et l'excellente qualité du vin du domaine.

[1] Kleine Kathedrale: Vorhalle zum Chefbüro
[2] Geschickte Inszenierung: Die Büros liegen an einem schmalen Durchgang

[1] Small cathedral: entrance hall to the executive office
[2] Clever setting: the offices are positioned along a narrow corridor

[1] Cathédrale en miniature : salle d'attente devant le bureau du chef
[2] Mise en scène ingénieuse: les bureaux donnent sur un passage étroit

Jan I. Shrem

Jan I. Shrem aus dem Libanon hat so gut wie die ganze Welt gesehen. Der erfolgreiche Kaufmann gilt als einer der bekanntesten Kunstsammler der Welt. Jetzt ist er kalifornischer Winzer von „Clos Pegase". Das sei ein Hinweis, wie er gern erklärt, „auf ein Werk Odilon Redons von 1890. Pegasus hat in der griechischen Mythologie jene Musen erweckt, die dem Wein das Leben gaben und die Poeten inspirierten." Dann fällt sein Blick auf einen wundervollen Kamin an der Stirnseite von Chefbüro und Weingut: „Ich brauche ihn nicht wirklich" sagt Shrem, der

Jan I. Shrem from Lebanon has as good as seen the entire world. The successful businessman is one of the most well-known art collectors in the world. Now he is a Californian wine-grower at the Clos Pegase. This is a reference, as he gladly explains, "to a work of Odilon Redon from 1890. In Greek mythology Pegasus roused the muses who gave life to wine and inspired the poets". Then his gaze falls upon a wonderful fireplace on the end wall of the executive office and estate: "I don't really need it" says Shrem who would have

Jan I. Shrem, qui vient du Liban, connaît pratiquement le monde entier. Cet homme d'affaires couronné de succès est considéré comme l'un des plus célèbres collectionneurs d'œuvres d'art du monde. Il est désormais le "vigneron" californien du Clos Pégase. Il explique volontiers: "le nom est inspiré d'une œuvre d'Odilon Redon datant de 1890. Dans la mythologie, Pégase a éveillé toutes les muses qui ont donné vie au vin et inspiré les poètes". Ensuite, son regard tombe sur une magnifique cheminée sur le pignon du bureau du directeur du domaine. "Je n'en ai vraiment pas besoin", dit Shrem, qui aurait aimé devenir lui-même architecte, "mais Michael Graves le désirait ainsi, afin de terminer à l'extérieur ce groupe de bâtiment, comme les autres angles, par une cheminée circulaire." Le Clos Pegase et Jan Shrem prouvent que la passerelle jetée entre vin, art et architecture

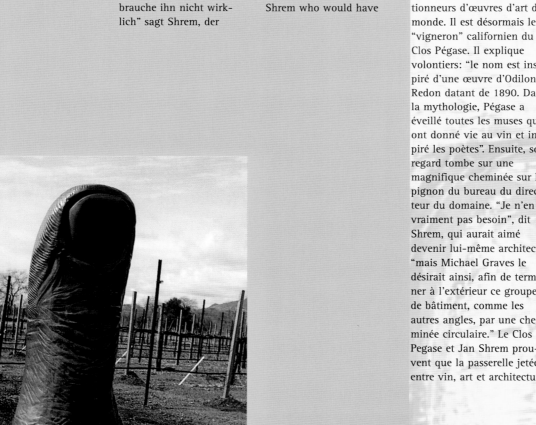

selbst gern Architekt geworden wäre, „aber Michael Graves wollte es so, um nach außen die Gebäudegruppe wie an den anderen Ecken mit einem runden Schornstein abschließen zu können". Mit Close Pegase und Jan Shrem beweist es sich, daß der Brückenschlag zwischen Wein, Kunst und Architektur keine leere Public Relation Phrase ist, sondern eine tiefere Bedeutung besitzt. Zwei kleine Erklärungen dazu: Im Keller reift nicht nur der Wein, sondern geben Künstler eine adäquate Performance. Die Weinetiketten werden jener Kunst gewidmet, die Shrem sammelt und die – sehr unprätentiös – gleich mit ausgestellt wird.

Zum Beispiel rechts: („Nu Chamarre", Jean Dubuffet, 1901 – 1988); links: Fingerplastik von César; Mitte: Ausschnitt aus der Glassammlung exquisiter Weinbehältnisse.

liked to become an architect himself, "but Michael Graves wanted it that way so as to be able to outwardly finish off the group of buildings with a round chimney, as at the other corners". Clos Pegase and Jan Shrem are proof that the link forged between wine, art and architecture is not merely an empty phrase used in public relations, but possesses a deeper significance. Two short explanations have to be added here; the cellar is not only a place where the wine matures; artists give an adequate performance. The wine labels are devoted to the art which Shrem collects and which is also - very unpretentiously - exhibited.

For example, right: ("Nu Chamarre", Jean Dubuffet, 1901-1988); left: finger sculpture by César; middle: detail from the glass collection of exquisite wine containers.

n'est pas un slogan de relation publique vide de sens, mais qu'elle repose sur une signification plus profonde. Deux petites explications à ce sujet: dans les caves, à côté du vin qui mûrit, des artistes donnent des représentations de qualité; les étiquettes des bouteilles du domaine sont dédiées aux différents arts que Shrem collectionne et qu'il expose ici, sans prétention.

Par exemple, à droite: "Nu Chamarre" de Jean Dubuffet (1901-1988); à gauche: le "pouce" géant du sculpteur César; au centre: une partie de la collection des verres et récipients à vins

Far Niente

Unterirdisch | Vermutlich ist es das kalifornische Weingut mit dem schönsten Namen: Far Niente: Süßes Nichtstun. Schon 1885 ebenfalls von Captain Hamden McIntyre, dem Architekten von Trefethen, entworfen, entspricht das Haus in etwa seinem dortigen Zwillingsbruder mit einer mehrgeschossigen Grundorganisation. Nur ist Far Niente anders als Trefethen geschickt in einen Hang gebaut und weitgehend aus Stein und Putz. Far Niente war bis in die siebziger Jahre seit der Prohibition geschlossen. Eigentümer Gil Nickel, Sproß einer Baumschuldynastie aus dem Osten der USA, hat 1978 neu begonnen. Nach außen wirkt Far Niente wie eine Mischung aus Farmhaus und Goldmine und ist unscheinbar, weil es die Topographie des Hügels gut ausnutzt. Die Schätze liegen tatsächlich unten im Berg. Seit der Rekonstruktion wird die neue Library of Wines, eine Art Präsenzkeller aller jemals produzierten Weine beständig aufgefüllt. Gil Nickel ist begeisterter Sammler von Oldtimern und hat in einer Remise ein kleines Automuseum eröffnet.

Underground | This Californian estate presumably has the nicest name: Far Niente – idle bliss. Designed in 1885 also by Captain Hamden McIntyre, the architect of Trefethen, the basic multi-storey organisation of the house roughly corresponds to that of its twin brother. Unlike Trefethen though, Far Niente is skilfully built on a slope and is, to a large degree, made of stone and plaster. Far Niente was closed from the time of the prohibition up until the seventies. The owner, Gil Nickel, scion of a tree-nursery dynasty from Eastern USA, began anew in 1978. From the outside Far Niente appears to be a mixture of a farmhouse and a goldmine and is inconspicuous in that it makes good use of the topography of the hill. The treasures do actually lie below in the hill. Since its reconstruction the new library of wines, a kind of reference cellar on all the wines ever produced, is constantly being restocked. Gil Nickel is an enthusiastic collector of old-timers and has opened a small car museum in an outbuilding.

En souterrain | Far Niente, est sans doute le domaine viticole californien qui porte le plus joli nom: il fait rêver à la douceur de ne rien faire. La décomposition sur plusieurs niveaux du bâtiment conçu en 1885 par le capitaine Hamden McIntyre, l'architecte de Trefethen, correspond à peu près à la délimitation des espaces attribués aux frères jumeaux auxquels il était destiné. Mais contrairement à Trefethen, Far Niente a été réalisé en une seule fois et presque uniquement en pierre et en plâtre. A cause de la Prohibition, Far Niente est resté fermé jusque dans les années 70. Son propriétaire Gil Nickel, descendant d'une dynastie de pépiniéristes de l'est des Etats-Unis, l'a rouvert en 1978. Vu de l'extérieur, Far Niente ressemble à un mélange de ferme et de mine d'or. Il reste assez discret, car il utilise bien la topographie de la colline. Les trésors sont en fait sous la montagne. Depuis la reconstruction, la nouvelle "bibliothèque du vin", une sorte de cave présentant tous les vins qui ont été produits, est remplie en permanence. Gil Nickel est aussi un collectionneur passionné de vieilles voitures et il a ouvert dans une remise un musée de l'automobile.

[2]

[3]

[1] Irrgarten: Kreuzgang
im Weinkeller
[2] Süßer Wein: Keller
der Schwestermarke
„Dolce"
[3] Unterirdisch: Degu-
station und „Bibliothek
des Weines"

[1] Maze: cloister in the
wine cellar
[2] Sweet wine: cellar of
the associated "Dolce"
label
[3] Underground: wine
tasting and "library of
wines"

[1] Labyrinthe: le cloître
de la cave à vin
[2] Vin doux: la cave de
la marque associée
"Dolce"
[3] En souterrain:
dégustation et "biblio-
thèque des vins"

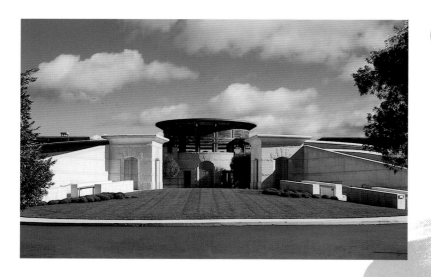

Opus One

Hochzeit der Kulturen | „Statement der Landschaft, Statement der Architektur", sagt der Architekt Scott Johnson. „Opus One ist klassisch und zeitgenössisch" sagt er auch. Man kann hinzufügen: Dank seiner beiden Väter Mondavi und Baron de Rothschild amerikanisch und europäisch gleichzeitig! Ein „Schmuckkästchen" wollten sie für ihren edlen Rotwein schaffen. Aus der Ferne vom Highway 29 aus nimmt Opus One allerdings ersteinmal die flüchtende Gestalt eines startenden Ufos ein; in der Anfahrt ähnelt das Haus dann eher einem Krematorium, das aus der Erde wächst. Die renommierten Landschaftsarchitekten Roysten, Hanamoto, Alley & Abey haben dem Bauwerk einen grünen Schutzwall umgelegt. Aus der Nähe differenziert sich dann der Eindruck, die gewichtigen natursteinernen Bauteile umrahmen eine zentrale Rotunde: eine eindeutige Referenz an die antike Klassik.

A marriage of cultures | "A landscape statement, an architectural statement", says the architect, Scott Johnson. In addition he states that "Opus One is classic and contemporary". One can also add that thanks to his two forebears, Mondavi and Baron de Rothschild, it is both American and European at the same time! They wanted to create a "jewellery box" for their precious, noble red wine. From Highway 29, however, Opus One at first takes on the fleeting form of a UFO taking off; on approaching the house it resembles more a crematorium growing out of the earth. The renowned landscape architects, Roysten, Hanamoto, Alley and Abey, put a green protective wall around the building. Close up, the impression becomes differentiated; the hefty parts of the building made from natural stone frame a central rotunda, a clear reference to Classical Antiquity.

Le mariage des cultures | "Mise en valeur du paysage, mise en valeur de l'architecture", dit l'architecte Scott Johnson. "Opus One est classique et contemporain", dit-il aussi. On peut ajouter qu'il est également américain et européen grâce à ses deux pères, Mondavi et le baron de Rothschild qui voulaient créer une "boîte à bijoux" pour leur noble vin rouge. Lorsqu'on roule sur l'autoroute 29, Opus One a de loin vaguement la forme d'un ovni en train de décoller. Quand on s'approche, il ressemble plutôt à un crématorium émergeant de la terre. Les architectes paysagistes Roysten, Hanamoto, Alley et Abey ont glissé autour de la construction un vert manteau protecteur. De près, les impressions se précisent: des éléments en pierre naturelle prépondérants entourent une rotonde centrale, une référence sans équivoque au classicisme antique.

[1]

[2]

Vorherige Seiten: Rätsel
– Startendes oder landendes Ufo?
[1] Im Zentrum: Eine
Rotunde gemahnt an
alte europäische Bautraditionen
[2] In der Rotunde führt
eine schwungvolle
Treppe in den Weinkeller

Previous pages: puzzle –
a UFO landing or taking
off?
[1] In the centre: a
rotunda reminiscent of
ancient European building traditions
[2] A sweeping staircase
in the rotunda leads into
the wine cellar

Pages précédentes: énigme
– un ovni en train de
décoller ou d'atterrir ?
[1] Au centre: une rotonde
qui évoque les anciennes
traditions de construction
européenne.
[2] Dans la rotonde, un
escalier plein d'élan
conduit dans la cave à vin

[1]

[2]

[1-2] Anspruchsvoll:
Totale und Detail des
Gästesalons
[3] Transparenz: Nur
eine Glaswand trennt
Degustation und Wein-
keller

[1-2] Sophisticated: the
complete guest salon
with detail
[3] Transparent: only a
glass wall separates the
tasting from the wine
cellar

[1-2] Plein d'élégance:
vue d'ensemble et détail
du salon des hôtes
[3] Transparence: seule
une paroi en verre sépa-
re dégustation et cave à
vin

[3]

Wesentliche Teile des Weingutes stecken unter der Erde, wie der Keller, der durch eine raumgreifende Treppe in der Rotunde erreichbar ist. Wie in einer Vitrine, hinter Glas reift hier Opus One. Das Schmuckkästchen ist gefunden. Platz für amerikanische Freizeit mit deftigem Barbecue ist oben unter der hölzernen Veranda, die an schattenbringende Vorbilder aus Arizona erinnert. „Hochzeit zweier Kulturen" nennen das die Architekten.

Essential parts of the estate are located underground, such as the cellar which is accessible via a spacious flight of stairs beneath the rotunda. Opus One matures here behind glass, as in a display case. The jewellery box is discovered. Above there is space for American leisure time with a good solid barbecue, beneath the wooden veranda reminiscent of shady examples from Arizona. The architects call it "a marriage of two cultures".

Des parties importantes du domaine sont enfouies sous la terre, comme le cellier, où l'on descend en empruntant un escalier monumental situé sous la rotonde. C'est là que mûrît l'Opus One, derrière du verre, comme dans une vitrine. C'est la "boîte à bijoux" dont rêvaient les propriétaires! Une base de loisirs à l'américaine, propice aux copieux barbecues, est située au-dessus, protégée par les ombrages d'une véranda en bois évoquant l'Arizona. Les architectes appellent cela: "le mariage de deux cultures".

[4]

[4] Geheimnisvoll: Wandkandelaber im Weinkeller
Nachfolgende Seiten: Großer Auftritt – Treppe zum Weinkeller, von ganz unten gesehen

[4] Mysterious: wall candelabra in the wine cellar
Following pages: grand entrance – stairs to the wine cellar, seen from the very bottom

[4] Ambiance mystérieuse: les appliques murales de la cave à vin
Pages suivantes: grande représentation – le départ de l'escalier menant à la cave à vin

Turnbull

rnbull

Wiedergeburt der Ursprünglichkeit |

William Turnbull aus San Francisco erkannte
in den frühen siebziger Jahren, daß die pure
Form der historischen amerikanischen
Scheune auch ein brauchbares Kleid für die
Betriebsgebäude eines Weinguts sein mußte.
Er lehnte sich an die erfolgreichen Vorgaben
der einige Meilen nördlich an der Pazifik-
küste gelegenen berühmten Freizeitanlage
Sea Ranch des Stararchitekten Charles
Moore an. Beide Bauwerke sind inzwischen
in die Jahre gekommen, deren Red-Cedar-
Kleider haben jedoch unter der Sonne
Kaliforniens würdevolle Patina angesetzt –
etwas Besseres kann man einem Haus nicht
wünschen!

The rebirth of simplicity | In the early
seventies William Turnbull from San Francisco recognised that the pure form of the
historical American barn must also be a use-
able mantle for the works buildings of an
estate. He followed the successful guidelines
of the famous Sea Ranch leisure centre by
the star architect, Charles Moore, situated a
few miles north of the Pacific coast. Both
buildings have aged in the meantime; their
red-cedar mantles have become coated with
a dignified patina under the Californian sun
– what more could one wish for a house!

Renaissance de la forme originelle |
William Turnbull, de San Francisco, s'est
rendu compte au début des années 70 que
la forme très pure de la grange américaine
historique pourrait être un vêtement pratique pour l'unité de production d'un domaine viticole. Il s'est appuyé sur les succès
de Sea Ranch, le célèbre complexe touristique de l'architecte Charles Moore, situé
à quelques miles vers le nord, sur la côte du
Pacifique. Entre temps, les deux réalisations
ont vieilli, mais leur vêture en red cedar a
pris sous le soleil de Californie une patine
vénérable. Que souhaiter de mieux à un
bâtiment?

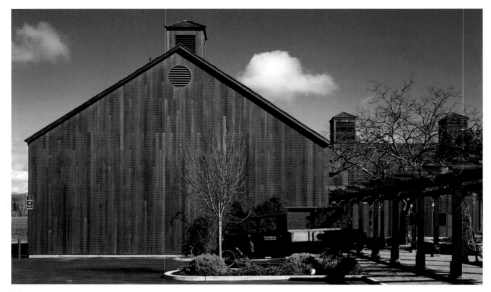

2

[1]

Einfach wie eine Scheune oder ein zeltartiges Hallenhaus faltet sich der Hauptbau über fast alle relevanten Bereiche und vor allem ein mächtiges hölzernes Hochregal auf, wo die Barriques lagern. Zum einzigen Schmuck am archaischen Ranch-Style werden zwei lichtbringende Lüftungstürmchen mitten auf dem Giebel. Inzwischen sind kleinere Nebengebäude hinzugefügt worden, die der perfekten Ausstrahlung der Grundfigur nicht schaden können. Genauso wenig wie die zahlreichen Epigonen in der Nachbarschaft: Aber eine einfache, logische und bildhafte Architektur setzt sich halt immer durch. Zumal sie beinah mit Bordmitteln selbst gezimmert werden kann.

As simply as with a barn or a tent-like hall, the main building unfolds over almost all relevant areas and, above all, over the immense, high, wooden shelving where the barriques are stored. The only decorative features of this ranch style are two light-transmissive ventilation turrets in the centre of the gable. Smaller annexes have since been added that cannot damage the perfect aura of the fundamental figure. Just as little as the numerous imitators in the neighbourhood: but simple, logical, pictorial architecture is always successful. Especially when it can almost be self-built.

Très simplement, comme une grange ou une halle en forme de tente, le bâtiment principal couvre presque toutes les fonctions importantes et avant tout les étagères en bois, hautes et imposantes, sur lesquelles sont entreposées les barriques. Les deux petites tours de ventilation au milieu du pignon qui laissent pénétrer la lumière naturelle constituent la seule parure de ce "ranch" archaïque. Entre temps, on a ajouté de petits bâtiments secondaires. Pas plus que les nombreuses copies sans caractère du voisinage, ils ne peuvent porter préjudice à l'image parfaite de la silhouette originale. Une architecture simple, logique et imagée s'impose toujours, sur-tout si elle peut être réalisée presque en auto-construction avec les moyens du bord.

[1] Wie ein Zelt: Weingut mit Lüftungstürmchen
[2] Hochgestapelt: Weinkeller mit Regal

[1] Tent-like: wine estate with ventilation turrets
[2] Stacked up: a wine cellar with shelves

[1] Comme une tente: un domaine viticole avec des petites tours de ventilation
[2] Superposition: les étagères de la cave à vin

Hess Collection

Collection

Kunst und Wein | Die Kunst des Weinmachens wird hier mit einem Museum der modernen Kunst konfrontiert. Der Schweizer Kaufmann Donald Hess schuf in der Kulisse eines der älteren Weingüter am Mount Vedder hoch über Napa ein doppeltes Museum: eines für den Wein, ein anderes für seine exzellente, sehr persönlich eingefärbte Kunstsammlung, die einen deutlichen Stich ins Europäische besitzt: Werke von Georg Baselitz, Gilbert & George, Per Kirkeby, Max Bill oder Fritz Glarner sind zu besichtigen. In den Räumen des historischen Weinhofes von 1903 wurden großzügige Galerieräume arrangiert.

Art and wine | Here the art of wine-making is confronted with a museum of modern art. The Swiss businessman, Donald Hess, created a double museum in the setting of one of the oldest estates on Mount Vedder high above Napa: one for the wine, the other for his excellent art collection, which has a very personal influence and a definite European slant: works by Georg Baselitz, Gilbert & George, Per Kirkeby, Max Bill or Fritz Glarner can be viewed here. Spacious gallery halls were arranged in the setting of the historical estate from the year 1903.

Quand le vin rencontre l'art moderne | Bien au-dessus de Napa, sur le Mont Vedder, l'homme d'affaires suisse Donald Hess a créé, près d'un des plus anciens domaines viticoles, un double musée consacré au vin et à sa remarquable collection d'art moderne. Très personnelle, elle est résolument tournée vers l'Europe et on peut y admirer des œuvres de Georg Baselitz, Gilbert & George, Per Kirkeby, Max Bill ou Fritz Glarner. Dans les coulisses de la ferme viticole historique de 1903, de vastes galeries ont été aménagées pour les accueillir.

[1] Ein neues Treppenhaus (mit Aufzug) dient als Verbindungsglied. Im Vorübergehen können die Besucher den Weinkeller besichtigen und sich im Audio-Video-Raum informieren. Dann mischen sich die Erfahrungen. Schon das Treppenhaus wird zur Galerie, am offensichtlichsten dort, wo die brennende Schreibmaschinen-Skulptur eines argentinischen Künstlers steht. Ganz in der Nähe schaut man durch ein Fenster in die akkurat aufgestellte Reihe von Gärtanks und Weinpresse.

A new stairwell (with lift) serves as a connecting joint. In passing, the visitors can inspect the wine cellar and gather information in the audio-video room. Experiences then merge. The stairwell turns into a gallery, most obviously at the spot where the burning typewriter sculpture of an Argentinian artist stands. In close proximity to this the visitor looks out of a window onto the meticulously installed row of fermentation tanks and wine presses.

Un nouvel escalier, flanqué d'un ascenseur, assure la liaison entre vin et art moderne. En l'empruntant, les touristes peuvent visiter le chai puis s'informer dans la salle vidéo. Ensuite, on mêle les expériences. L'escalier est déjà une galerie d'art. C'est particulièrement sensible à l'emplacement de la "machine à écrire en feu", une sculpture d'un artiste argentin. Près de là, une ouverture offre une vue sur une rangée de citernes à fermentation et de pressoirs rigoureusement alignés.

[1] Nahtstelle: Ein neues Treppenhaus mit einem transparenten Aufzug erschließt die beiden „Museen" des Weines und der Kunst in den Altbauten des Weinguts

[1] The seam: a new stairwell with a transparent lift provides access to both the museum of wine and museum of art in the old buildings of the estate

[1] Espace de rencontre: un nouvel escalier et un ascenseur transparent donnent accès aux deux "musées" situés dans les anciens bâtiments du domaine: le musée du vin et l'exposition d'art

[1]

In der Galerie des dritten Stockwerks, in der unter mächtigem Dach Großformate gezeigt werden, wird ein Schaufenster, das den Blick zur Flaschenfüllanlage freigibt, beinahe auch zum Kunstwerk. Der Schweizer Architekt Beat A.H. Jordi (zusammen mit Richard MacRae) hat ein farbharmonisches, zurückhaltendes Ensemble entwickelt: ein sanfter Weiterbau in alter Bausubstanz. Allein die Treppenanlage mit ihren Geländern und dem Aufzug ist ein bißchen „kräftiger" ausgefallen. Kunst und Wein zu kombinieren, war eine Idee Hess' Ehefrau Joana. Das Konzept ist aufgegangen – weil auf beiden Feldern hier höchste Qualität geboten wird.

In the gallery on the third floor in which large formats are shown below a massive roof, a display window permitting a view of the bottling plant almost becomes a work of art in itself. The Swiss architect, Beat AH Jordi (together with Richard MacRae) developed a colourfully harmonious, restrained ensemble: a modest continuation of building based on the old substance. The stairs alone with their galleries and lift have turned out a little more powerful. The idea of combining art and wine came from Hess' wife, Joana. The concept dawned on her – because high quality was being offered here in both these fields.

Dans les galeries du troisième étage, où des œuvres de grand format sont présentées sous un toit imposant, une vitrine libérant la vue vers la mise en bouteille devient elle aussi presque une œuvre d'art. L'architecte suisse Beat A.H. Jordi (associé à Richard Mac Rae) a développé là un ensemble harmonieux et discret, avec un agrandissement qui s'inscrit en douceur dans le bâti ancien. Seul le groupe formé par les liaisons verticales, et en particulieer le garde-corps de l'escalier et l'ascenseur, sont un peu trop massifs. Combiner l'art et le vin était une idée de la femme de Hess, Joana. Le concept s'est épanoui et on propose ici la meilleure qualité dans les deux domaines.

[2]

[3]

Vorherige Seiten:
Zweimal „Kunst": die zen-
trale Flaschenfüllanlage
und ein Gemälde im Stil
des Schweizer Realismus
[1] Treppenhaus mit
Durchblick zum Gärkeller
[2] Großzügig: Galerie-
etage für Skulpturen
[3] Rundum: Bartresen
für die Degustation

Previous pages: two
examples of "art": the
central bottling plant and
a painting in the style of
Swiss realism
[1] Stairwell with a view
of the fermentation cellar
[2] Spacious: gallery level
for sculptures
[3] All around: bar coun-
ters for tasting

Pages précédentes: deux
formes d' "art" – les installations centrales
d'embouteillage et une
peinture dans le style
du réalisme suisse
[1] Cage d'escalier avec
vue sur la cave de fer-
mentation
[2] Généreuse: la galerie
pour les sculptures
[3] Les comptoirs de bar
pour la dégustation

Robert Sinskey
Vineyards

Weinbasilika | Direkt am Silverado Trail steht ein Weingut, so wie es sich Europäer wohl gern vorstellen wollen; aus silberglänzendem Holz und rauhem Gestein, ein Ort, wo die Kakteen gern blühen. Nahezu lässig querab in den Berg gestellt, ein Schiff, das gerade festmachen will. Es ist ein gefälliger Stil made in Arizona oder Texas, und das schmeckt nach wildem Westen. Innen ist die Stimmung eher ruhig und getragen und der Großteil der Fässer verschwindet in einem riesigen Tunnelsystem im Berg. Architekt ist der Kirchenbauer Oscar Leidenfrost. Vielleicht ist das eine griffige Erklärung dafür, daß die Anlage wie eine dreischiffige Kirche wirkt. Das mittlere Schiff ist beinahe gotisch hochgereckt, dort sind alle wichtigen Touristeneinrichtungen versammelt. Besonders beeindruckend ist die Show-Küche, in der bisweilen Kochstudios fürs Fernsehen aufgezeichnet werden. Robert Sinskey gilt als progressiver Abenteurer, seine Mischung aus Ponderosa und Kirche lockt Sinnesgenossen an.

Church of Wine | Directly on the Silverado Trail is an estate exactly as Europeans would like to imagine it; the silvery gleam of the wood and the rough stone - a place where the cacti tend to like to flower. A ship, placed almost carelessly crossways on the hill, is just about to moor. It is a pleasant style made in Arizona or Texas and with a taste of the wild west. Inside the atmosphere is more serene and stately and the majority of the barrels disappear into a huge tunnel system in the hill. The architect is Oscar Leidenfrost, the church architect. Maybe this is a useful explanation for the fact that the estate takes on the appearance of a church with three naves. The middle nave is almost Gothic; all the important tourist facilities are gathered here. Particularly impressive is the show kitchen in which cooking studios are recorded now and again for television. Robert Sinskey is known as a progressive adventurer; his mixture of Ponderosa and church attracts "like-minded" people.

La basilique du vin | Au milieu du chemin de grande randonnée "Silverado trail", il existe un domaine viticole comme les européens l'imaginent, construit en pierres rugueuses et en bois gris argenté, dans un lieu où les cactus aiment fleurir. Il ressemble à un bateau, nonchalamment planté à travers la montage, qui s'apprête à prendre le large. Ce style aimable, qui évoque l'Arizona ou le Texas, a un goût de Far West. A l'intérieur, l'ambiance est plutôt calme et solennelle. La plupart des tonneaux sont dissimulés dans un immense complexe souterrain disposé sous la montagne. L'architecte, Oscar Leidenfrost, est un spécialiste des églises. Cela explique sans doute pourquoi sa réalisation rappelle un sanctuaire à trois nefs. Très élevée, la nef centrale, où sont rassemblées toutes les installations touristiques, est d'inspiration gothique. La cuisine de démonstration, où sont tournées de temps en temps des émissions culinaires pour la télévision, est particulièrement impressionnante. Robert Sinskey a la réputation d'être un aventurier progressiste, son mélange d'église et de Ponderosa attire ceux qui lui ressemblent.

[1]

[2]

[1+3] Als wär's ein
Stück Wilder Westen:
Rauhe Schale für den
Weinbauern
[2] Zugang mit Überra-
schung: der Weg in die
„Basilika"

[1+3] As if it were a
piece of the wild west:
Rough skin for the wine
growers
[2] Entrance with a sur-
prise: the pathway to the
"Basilica"

[1+3] Comme au Far
West: une coquille
rugueuse pour les
vignerons
[2] Un accès qui réserve
des surprises: le chemin
vers la "basilique"

[1]

[1] Showküche
[2] Sakraler Eindruck:
die Halle mit Empfangs-
tresen

[1] Show kitchen
[2] Sacral impression: the
hall with reception coun-
ters

[1] La cuisine de
démonstration
[2] Impression sacrée : le
hall avec les comptoirs
d'accueil

Artesa

Huldigung der Landschaft | Wie die moderne Spielart einer Trutzburg, vergleichbar mit stolzen Burgen des Rheinlandes, thront die zweistufige, abgestumpfte Pyramide über dem südlichen Talausgang. Bei günstigem Wetter kann man in der Ferne die Bay und ihre Metropole San Francisco am Horizont erkennen. Das Sekt- und Weingut, das es in der spanischen Heimat zum königlichen Hoflieferanten gebracht hat, wird durch eine gewundene alpine Straße erschlossen, die den Hügel umfährt: Das landscaping steht hier unter dem Thema „alles fließt". Die Basis des Bauwerks steckt hinter einem Erdwall mit Grasboden. Dort unten wird Weißwein spanischer Prägung und Sekt zur Blüte gebracht, gewachsen auf dem Terrain ehemals spanischer Kolonien. Die Spitze des aufgesetzten künstlichen Berges, geschaffen vom katalanischen Architekten Domingo Triary aus Barcelona, 1991, signalisiert nach außen, daß Gäste hoch willkommen sind, denn der gläserne Eingang oben

Homage to the landscape | Like a modern version of a castle built to besiege an enemy castle, comparable to the majestic castles of the Rhineland, the two-tier, "blunted" pyramid stands in solitary splendour above the southern end of the valley. If the weather conditions are favourable, the bay can be made out in the distance as well as its metropolis, San Francisco, on the horizon. The champagne and wine estate, which has become royal purveyor to the court in the Spanish homeland, is accessible by a winding alpine road running around the hill: the landscaping here is based on the theme "everything flows". The base of the building stands behind a grass-covered earth wall with. Here below the the Spanish-type white wine and the champagne is cultivated, grown on the land previously belonging to Spanish colonies. The tip of the artificial hill, created in 1991 by the Catalan architect, Domingo Triary from Barcelona, outwardly signals that guests are highly welcome due to the cleverly conspicuous setting of the

Hommage au paysage | Vision moderne et ludique d'une citadelle, comparable aux fiers châteaux forts de la vallée du Rhin, une pyramide tronquée à deux degrés trône au-dessus de l'extrémité sud de Napa valley. Par beau temps, on peut apercevoir à l'horizon la baie et la métropole de San Francisco. Le domaine, qui produit du vin et du champagne, a réussi à devenir fournisseur de la cour royale espagnole. On y accède par une route de montagne en lacets qui contourne la montagne. L'aménagement du paysage est tout en douceur. La base de la construction est cachée derrière un rempart de terre planté. Dessous, on fait fleurir du champagne et un vin blanc à l'estampille de l'Espagne, sur les terres d'une ancienne colonie espagnole. La pointe de cette montagne artificielle, créée en 1991 par l'architecte catalan Domingo Triary, de Barcelone, est un signal vers l'extérieur: il souhaite la bienvenue aux visiteurs. Très bien mise en scène, l'entrée vitrée sur le plateau, avec ses colonnes jumelles, ne risque

[1]

auf dem Plateau ist mit seinen Zwillings-
säulen so geschickt inszeniert, daß er un-
übersehbar ist. Dort und mit einem spitz-
winkligen dreieckigen Glaserker mit getön-
ten Scheiben scheint der Bau aus dem
Berggefängnis ausbrechen zu wollen. Der
Umgang mit architektonischen Statements
ist kurz und knapp – statt dessen wird gehuldigt, was den Wein hier erst gedeihen
läßt – die fruchtbare Erde in hügeliger Landschaft. Auf dem Top sind Weinstöcke der
Sorte Cabernet Sauvignon angepflanzt.

Ganz anders innen. Dort findet zwischen
kräftigen Säulen und elegantem Holzfußbo-
den eine Leistungsschau des modernen spanischen Möbeldesigns statt. Doch im Kern
herrscht Ruhe. Es lockt ein mediterranes
schattiges Atrium mit Wasserbecken: in der
Mitte eine stolze Madonnenstatue.

glass entrance with its twin pillars on the
plateau above. Here and with a sharp-cor-
nered, triangular glass oriel with tinted windows, the building appears to want to break
out of this prison of a hill. Any allusion to
architectonic statements here is short and
concise – instead homage is paid to that
which allows the wine to thrive in the first
place – the fertile soil in an undulating
landscape. Vines of the Cabernet Sauvignon
variety have been planted on top.

The interior is completely different. Here,
between massive pillars and an elegant
wooden floor, is an exhibition of modern
Spanish furniture design. And yet silence
reigns at the core of the building. A shady,
Mediterranean atrium with its pool beckons:
an impressive statue of the Madonna
stands in the centre.

pas de passer inaperçue. Là, une excroissan-
ce en verre teinté aux angles aigus donne
l'impression que le bâtiment veut sortir de la
montagne qui l'emprisonne. Le parti architectural se résume à un seul principe: ici, on
préfère rendre hommage à ce qui fait pous-
ser le vin, la terre fertile de la colline au
sommet de laquelle sont plantés des ceps de
cabernet sauvignon.

L'intérieur est tout différent. Là, entre
des colonnes massives et un parquet élégant, est exposé du mobilier espagnol con-
temporain. Au cœur du domaine, le calme
règne. D'inspiration méditerranéenne, un
atrium ombragé et son bassin attirent
les visiteurs. Au centre, trône une superbe
statue de la Madone.

Vorherige Seiten: In den
Berg gebaut: Ausblick
und Ausgang in die
freie Landschaft
[1] Designerkunst:
Treppendetail in der
Halle

Previous pages: built into
the mountain: view of
and way out into the
open countryside
[1] Designer art: detail of
the hall stairs

Pages précédentes:
construit dans les mon-
tages – vue et ouverture
sur le paysage
[1] L'art du designer :
détail de l'escalier du
hall

[2]

[3]

[4]

[2] Erde und Wasser: Gehuldigt wird, was dem Wein nutzt
[3-4] Skulpturengarten: Kunst on Top und in freier Natur

[2] Soil and water: homage is paid to that which is useful to the wine
[3-4] Sculpture garden: art on top and in open nature

[2] La terre et l'eau: on rend hommage à se qui sert le vin
[3-4] Jardin de sculptures: l'art au meilleur niveau et au milieu de la nature

[1]

[2]

[3]

[4]

[1-4] Leistungsschau:
Die besten spanischen
Designer präsentieren
Möbel für Büro- und
Gästeräume
Nachfolgende Seiten:
Im Herzen – Patio mit
Madonnenstatue

[1-4] The best Spanish
designers present furni-
ture for the office and
guest areas
Following pages: at the
heart – patio with statue
of the Madonna

[1-4] Exposition: les meilleurs designers espagnols
présentent leurs meubles
pour bureaux et espaces
d'accueil
Pages suivantes: au cœur
du domaine – le patio
avec une statue de vierge
à l'enfant

Dominus

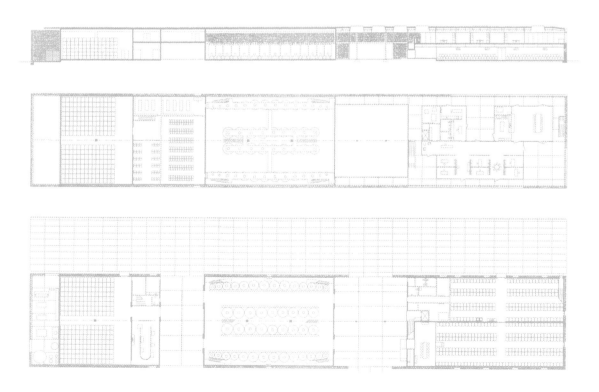

minus

Europäischer Ideentransfer | Der französische Direktor des Château Petrus in Pomerol beauftragte die Schweizer Architekten Herzog und de Meuron ein „kalifornisches Château" zu entwickeln; es wurde das erste Bauwerk der Schweizer Erfolgsarchitekten in den USA, weitere werden auf Grund der Qualität von Dominus Estate folgen. Es entstand ein Unikat einer Architektur, die sich einerseits als unauffälliger Bestandteil des Ortes versteht und selbstverständlich aus einem Weinberg wie eine Mauer herauswachsen sollte. Hartnäckig hält sich das Gerücht, daß manche Bewohner von Yountville monatelang das neue Weingut gar nicht richtig wahrgenommen hätten.

European transfer of ideas | The French director of the Château Petrus in Pomerol commissioned the Swiss architects, Herzog and de Meuron, to build "a discrete winery"; it was the first building in the USA by these successful architects, others would follow on the basis of the success they achieved with the Dominus Estate. A unique piece of architecture was created, which on the one hand sees itself as an unobtrusive element of the environment, growing naturally like a wall out of a vineyard. The rumour still circulates that residents of Yountville failed to really notice the new estate for months.

Transfert d'idées européennes | Le directeur français du Château Petrus à Pomerol a confié aux célèbres architectes suisses Herzog et de Meuron la conception d'un "Château discret en californie". Dominus Estate était la première réalisation de ces architectes à succès aux Etats-Unis; d'autres doivent suivre grâce à sa réussite. Herzog et de Meuron ont créé là une architecture originale, perçue comme un élément discret du paysage; un mur qui sort comme naturellement des vignes. Le bruit court que des mois après sa mise en service certains habitants de Yountville n'avaient pas encore remarqué le nouveau domaine.

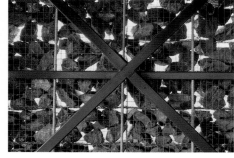

[1]   [2]   [3]

Andererseits haben die Architekten dann doch einen selbstbewußten Solitär mit archaischer, fast ägyptisierender Wirkung geschaffen. Optisch wird dieser Effekt durch zwei rechteckige Durchlässe erhöht. Einer davon liegt genau in der Achse der Zufahrtsstraße (aber nicht in der Gebäudemitte!) und rahmt wie ein Passepartout einen Landschaftsausschnitt mit Weinstöcken ein. Von der Straße her gesehen, liegt Dominus eigentlich dunkel und stumm in den Weinbergen, bei sanfter Annäherung verwandelt sich die Szene: Dominus leuchtet plötzlich

On the other hand, the architects did indeed create a self-confident solitaire with an archaic, almost Egyptian-like effect. Optically, this effect is heightened by two rectangular openings. One of these lies directly on the axis of the access road (but not in the centre of the building!) and like a passepartout frames a vine-covered landscape detail. Seen from the road, Dominus actually lies dark and silent in the vineyards, yet on gently approaching it the scene transforms:

En même temps, les architectes ont réussi à créer un "solitaire" sûr de lui, à l'aura archaïque, presque égyptienne. Cet effet est visuellement renforcé par la présence de deux brèches rectangulaires. La première, située dans l'axe du chemin d'accès (mais pas au milieu du bâtiment!), crée un cadre qui met en valeur le paysage viticole. De la route, Dominus Estate semble reposer, sombre et muet, au milieu des vignes. La scène se transforme au fur et à mesure

Vorherige Seiten: Back to earth – der Baukörper wirkt streng, archaisch und fremd
[1-3] Mauerwerksbau I: Basaltsteine in einer Konstruktion aus Schanzkörben bilden die äußere Schale der Fassadenkonstruktion

Previous pages: back to earth – the building has a severe, archaic, foreign appearance
[1-3] Masonry I: basalt in a construction "loose" cement-free makes up the outer shell of the facade

Pages précédentes: retour à la terre – le corps de bâtiment semble rigide, archaïque et étranger
[1-3] Maçonnerie I: la coque extérieure de la façade est en blocs de basalte, maintenus par un treillis métallique

[4]

[5]

und die Steinmauer wird transparent. Eine Folge der ebenso durchdachten wie uralten Fassadenkonstruktion, die dem Bau von alpinen Stützmauern entlehnt wurde und bei der Basaltsteine in Schanzkörbe geschichtet werden, ohne die Zwischenräume zu füllen. So dringt Licht von innen nach außen, wie selbstverständlich auch umgekehrt.

Dominus suddenly glows and the stone wall becomes transparent. This is achieved by an ancient, yet just as equally thought-through, method of constructing a facade, borrowed from the art of constructing alpine supporting walls in which basalt is stacked without filling in the spaces in between. Thus light from the inside is forced outwards, and vice versa of course.

qu'on s'approche: le domaine s'illumine soudain et le mur en pierre devient transparent. Très bien conçue, cette succession de façades est inspirée d'une technique déjà éprouvée, empruntée aux murs de soutènement alpins. Les blocs de basalte superposés sont maintenus par une structure métallique. La lumière peut ainsi filtrer de l'intérieur vers l'extérieur, et bien sûr inversement.

[4-5] Mauerwerksbau II: An einigen Stellen wird sichtbar, daß hinter der Außenmauer oft noch eine zweite Wandscheibe aus Beton, Glas oder Stahl steht

[4-5] Masonry II: In some places it becomes evident that there is often a second wall segment made of concrete, glass or steel behind the external wall

[4-5] Maçonnerie II: à certains endroits, on peut découvrir une deuxième peau en béton, en verre ou en acier derrière le mur extérieur

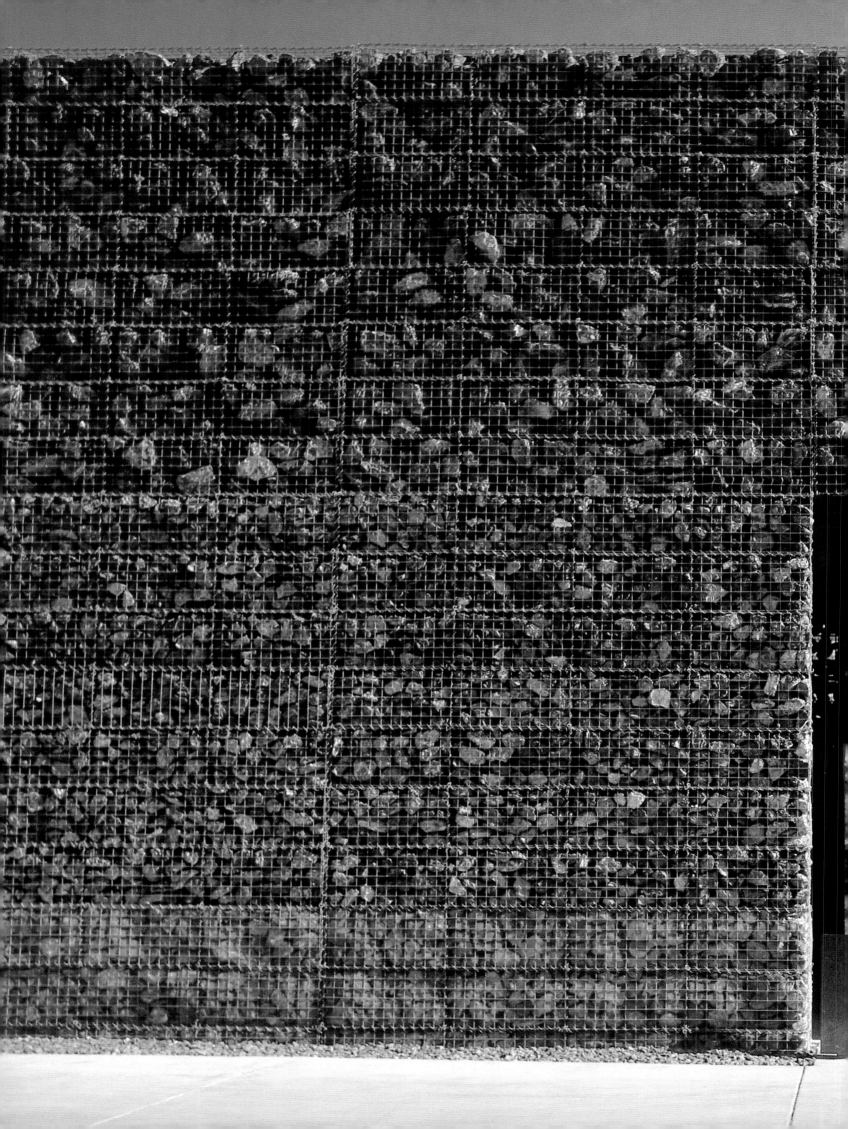

[1]

Vorherige Seiten: Die
Durchfahrt präsentiert
die kalifornische Wein-
landschaft wie in einem
Passepartout
[1-3] Perfekte Detaillier-
kunst: Treppen, Fenster,
Türen und Einbauten
wirken im Gegensatz
zur äußeren Hülle leicht,
ja fast ein bißchen fragil

Previous pages: the jour-
ney through the Californ-
ian wine countryside is
presented as if in a
passe-partout
[1-3] Perfect detail: stairs,
windows, doors and fit-
tings appear, in contrast
to the external shell, light
and almost slightly fragile

Pages précédentes: la
traversée présente le
paysage des vignobles
californiens comme à
travers un cadre
[1-3] Perfection dans
l'art du détail: en
contraste avec l'enve-
loppe extérieure, esca-
liers, fenêtres, portes et
aménagements sem-
blent légers et presque
un peu fragiles

[2]

[3]

Diese Außenwand ist Teil einer mehrschichtigen Wandkonstruktion, das heißt, dort, wo es notwendig ist, liegt Beton dahinter, Luken und Lüftungsanlage werden durch die Außenmauer gut kaschiert – in jedem Fall herrschen in den Kellern und Gärkellern optimale klimatische Bedingungen. Der „steinerne Container", in dem auf 3000 Quadratmetern alle Belange einer Winery untergebracht sind, ist links und rechts der Hauptdurchfahrt auf zwei Etagen so organisiert, daß links Cuvier und Lager, rechts unten der Weinkeller und oben die Administration liegen.

This external wall is part of a multi-layered wall construction. In other words, cement lies behind where necessary, the trap-doors and ventilation system are well concealed by the external wall - in any case, the climatic conditions in the cellars and tankroom are optimum. All the requisites of a winery are accommodated in the 3000 square metre "stone container": this is organised to the left and right of the main thoroughfare on two levels such that to the left lie the tankroom and storage and to the right lie the barrel cellars, below, and administration, above.

Cette façade fait partie d'un mur extérieur complexe: là où c'est nécessaire, il est doublé par du béton, les ouvertures et les bouches d'aération étant dissimulées par la peau minérale. Dans le cellier et les caves, les conditions climatiques sont optimales. Le "container en pierre", dans lequel toutes les fonctions d'une ferme viticole ont trouvé leur place sur 3 000 mètres carrés, est organisé sur deux étages, de chaque côté de l'accès principal: à gauche, cuvier et entrepôt; à droite, le cellier au niveau bas et l'administration au dessus.

[1]

Die Büros und Labors werden durch eine zweite Wand aus Glas und Stahl geschützt, die so elegant ist, wie es Amerika seit Mies van der Rohe nicht mehr gesehen hat. Die nahezu euphorische Würdigung dieses Bauwerks in der Welt der Architektur ist berechtigt und hat viele Gründe, denn Herzog und de Meuron haben die Themen „Alte Welt/ Neue Welt" oder „alte Bauaufgabe/neue Interpretation" auf ihre sensible, zeitgemäße Art bewältigt: Die ungebändigte Natur Amerikas trifft in den Weinbergen am Highway

The offices and laboratories are protected by a second wall of glass and steel, which is more elegant than anything America has seen since Mies van der Rohe. The virtually euphoric recognition of the building in the architectural world is justified and based on numerous reasons; Herzog and de Meuron dealt with the themes "old world/new world" or "old construction task/new interpretation" in their sensitive, contemporary way. In the vineyards along the highway America's untamed nature meets the culture

Les bureaux et les laboratoires sont protégés par un deuxième mur en métal et verre, si élégant que l'Amérique n'en avait pas vu de semblable depuis Mies van der Rohe. L'hommage presque euphorique que le monde de l'architecture a rendu à cette réalisation est mérité à plusieurs titres. Á leur manière sensible et contemporaine, Herzog et de Meuron ont maîtrisé ici l'équilibre entre l'ancien et le nouveau monde et apporté une interprétation contemporaine à un ancien type constructif. Ils ont thématisé la

[2]

[3]

auf die Kultur einer Gesellschaft, die immer in Bewegung ist. Nichts anderes haben die Architekten hier thematisiert. Und: Eine „Fabrik" von 3000 Quadratmetern mit dem Selbstverständnis einer Mauer zu bauen, zeigt die neuen Möglichkeiten einer Landarchitektur auf, die nicht weit entfernt von Landart liegt.

of a society that is constantly moving. This alone was used here as a central theme by the architects. Furthermore, building a 3000 square metre "factory" with the casualness of building a wall demonstrates the new possibilities of rural architecture, which are not far removed from Land art.

nature sauvage de l'Amérique rencontrant dans les vignobles, près de l'autoroute, la culture d'une société toujours en mouvement. En traitant une "usine" de 3 000 mètres carrés comme un simple mur, ils ont aussi démontré les nouvelles possibilités d'une architecture paysagée qui n'est pas très éloignée du Land art.

Vorherige Seiten und [1-3]: Auf den Spuren von Mies van der Rohe – Glas-Stahlwände, die die Büroräume einfassen

Previous pages and [1-3]: On the tracks of Mies van der Rohe – glass-steel walls which border the office areas

Pages précédentes et [1-3]: sur les traces de Mies van der Rohe - murs-rideaux en verre et en acier qui entourent les espaces de bureaux

Das Handwerk des Weinmachens

Peter C. Hubschmid

Moses schrieb das erste Weingesetz

In den Tontafeln Hammurabis, der 1800 Jahre vor Christus das babylonische Reich gründete, ist von Weinhandel Fachgeschäften die Rede. In den Gesetzen Moses gibt es bereits detaillierte Vorschriften für den Anbau von Trauben und das Weinmachen. Sie sind, was etwa die Hygiene bei der Weinbereitung angeht, vorbildlich und noch heute die Grundlage für die Kelterung und den Ausbau koscheren Weins.

Bei Griechen und Römern hatte Wein einen hohen Stellenwert. Die Amphoren, in denen er transportiert wurde, fand man längs der Schiffahrtsrouten der Antike auf dem Grund des Mittelmeeres. Plinius der Ältere befaßt sich in seiner Naturgeschichte ausführlich mit dem Weinbau - aus eigener Beobachtung, aber auch durch Rückgriff auf die Schriften Varros, der seinerseits vom Karthager Mago gelernt hatte.

Schon damals ging es um Qualität: Cato der Ältere schreibt in seinem Buch über die Landwirtschaft, daß Trauben völlig reif gelesen werden sollen, damit der daraus gekelterte Wein nicht seinen guten Ruf verliere. Und er mahnte zur Sauberkeit, damit der Wein nicht zu Essig werde.

Als neuartige „griechische Presse" beschreibt Plinius die Torggel, jene imposante Kelter, die ihren Druck mit einem Baumstamm als Hebel und einem gewaltigen, an einer Spindel hängenden Steingewicht erzeugt. Sie ist in ihrer sanften Wirkung auf das Preßgut bis heute nicht übertroffen.

Nach dem, was wir von den Weinen der Griechen und Römer wissen, würden sie uns, die wir samtigen, körperreichen Cabernet, filigranen Riesling und fruchtigen Chardonnay schätzen, kaum schmecken. Es waren oxidierte, mit allerlei Gewürzen und der Haltbarkeit dienenden Zusätzen versetzte Kreszenzen, die man nur mit Wasser verdünnt genießen konnte.

Die großzügig angelegte Villa, das Landgut der Römer, ist das älteste uns bekannte Beispiel eines für die Erzeugung von Wein (neben anderen Produkten der Landwirtschaft) bestimmten Baumusters. Der von Wohn- und Wirtschaftsgebäuden umgebene Hof bildete das Zentrum des ländlichen Lebens. Zur Erntezeit wurden dort die Karren entladen, die die Trauben zur Kelter brachten. Als Weinbehälter dienten Amphoren. Fässer wurden in Rom erst im dritten Jahrhundert unserer Zeitrechnung üblich.

artig und kostbar macht. Und in Deutschland kann selbst strenger Frost gefragt sein, wenn Eiswein entstehen soll, der aus gefrorenen Trauben gekeltert wird. Daß der sonnigste Hang der beste ist, gilt an Mosel und Rhein ebenso wie in Burgund, aber in Cassis an der französischen Riviera gedeihen die feinsten Weißen an den Nordhängen - wie es schon der Karthager Mago für seine nordafrikanische Heimat empfahl.

Ein Rebstock kann mit den Wurzeln nur eine bestimmte Menge Mineralstoffe aus dem Boden lösen und in die Früchte befördern. Diese sind es, die den Charakter eines Weins bestimmen. Sehr alte Rebstöcke bringen nur noch wenige, dafür geschmacksintensive Trauben hervor. Um den gleichen Effekt bei neu angelegten Weinbergen zu erzielen, pflanzt man heute mehr Stöcke je Hektar. Und schneidet die Reben im Winter, vor dem Austrieb, so kurz, daß jede nur wenig Frucht trägt. So bekommt man mehr Wurzeln pro Traube - und eine Geschmacksintensität, wie es sie früher nur bei Lesegut von sehr alten Stöcken gab. Denn weniger ist mehr beim Wein. Begnügt man sich mit einem geringeren Ertrag, also weniger Wein pro Hektar, bekommt man Wein mit mehr „Trockenextrakt", also mehr Charakter und Geschmack.

Die Grundregeln für große Weine

Im Mittelalter waren es vor allem die Klöster, die den Weinbau weiterentwickelten, etwa die Benediktiner im burgundischen Cluny, die Zisterzienser in Eberbach im Rheingau. Die Mönche erforschten und verbesserten den Anbau der Reben und die Kellertechnik und schufen dabei die Grundlage für den modernen Weinbau.

Das Weinmachen - winemaking - als Begriff ist amerikanischen Ursprungs und umfaßt im engeren Sinne die Verarbeitung der Trauben bis zur Flaschenfüllung. In der Neuen Welt (weinmäßig zählen neben Amerika Australien, Neuseeland und Südafrika dazu) ist die Einstellung zum Weinmachen pragmatisch geprägt, nach dem Grundsatz: Wie können wir den besten Wein machen? In Europa dagegen bestimmt überwiegend die Tradition, welche Rebsorten gepflanzt und wie die Weine ausgebaut werden.

Die Grundregeln aber sind überall die gleichen: Gute, und erst recht große Weine entstehen zunächst im Weinberg. Die Geburt eines großen Weins beginnt mit dem Pflanzen eines Rebstocks an einem Platz, der der jeweiligen Traubensorte die besten Bedingungen bietet. Dazu gehören die Zusammensetzung des Bodens und das Angebot an Wasser, die Summe der jährlichen Sonnenstunden, die Temperaturdifferenz zwischen Tag und Nacht, Sommer und Winter, die Brise, die den Nebel vertreibt oder eben der Nebel, der - etwa im Sauternes-Gebiet -, aufzieht und den Trauben die Edelfäule beschert, die die daraus gekelterten Weine einzig-

Die Rebe als Gestalterin der Kulturlandschaft

Der Rebstock ist neben dem Ölbaum und dem Getreide eine
der ersten Kulturpflanzen, die Landschaften bestimmt haben.
Damit aus reifen, gesunden Trauben der bestmögliche Wein
entsteht, muß das Lesegut unversehrt und so frisch wie
möglich verarbeitet werden. Die Kellerei muß sich also nahe
beim Weinberg befinden. Weingut und Kellerei inmitten der
Rebberge sind seit Jahrhunderten das Ideal für die
Erzeugung großer Weine. Ein Bild, das in vielfacher Form
auf Etiketten aus aller Welt auftaucht.

Die Anlagen für die Kelterung müssen groß genug sein,
um in wenigen Wochen die Ernte des Jahres zu bewältigen.
Haben die Trauben den optimalen Reifepunkt erreicht, bleiben nur ein paar Tage, um sie in diesem Zustand zu lesen.
Die Kelteranlagen gehören zu den kostspieligsten Investitionen auf einem Weingut, und sie stehen mindestens elf
Monate des Jahres still.

Für Annahmestationen, Entrapper und Pressen, Pumpen,
Leitungen und Tanks ist heute Edelstahl das bevorzugte
Material. Seine kühle, mattglänzende Ästhetik bestimmt das
Erscheinungsbild einer modernen Kellerei. Er ist leicht sau-
ber zu halten und erleichtert die Einhaltung der Hygienenor-
men, er geht mit dem Wein, insbesondere dessen Säuren,
keine Reaktionen oder Verbindungen ein. Inox-Tanks er-
leichtern die für eine optimale Gärführung unerläßliche
Temperatursteuerung - meist muß gekühlt, seltener mal auch
erwärmt werden.

Um aus dem Lesegut das Beste zu machen, müssen nicht
nur Trauben, sondern auch Maische, Most und Wein so
schonend wie möglich behandelt werden. Fließen lassen ist

besser als pumpen. Darum werden Kellereien, wenn möglich, so angelegt, daß die Schwerkraft den Transport von einer Station zur nächsten besorgt. Für die besten Weine wird oft nur der Freilauf- oder Vorlaufmost verwendet, die „tête de cuvée", die ohne Pressen, nur durch das eigene Gewicht aus der Maische abfließt. Für ein optimales Ergebnis wichtig ist die selektive Lese und Verarbeitung der Trauben: Jede Traube muß im Zustand der besten Reife geerntet werden; manche Sorten reifen früh, andere spät. Auch von Lage zu Lage gibt es Unterschiede. Die „Cuvée", die Komposition der Sorten, findet erst nach der Gärung statt.

Das Faß als Maß des Kellers

Für den Ausbau, also die weitere Reifung des jungen Weins vor der Abfüllung, spielen vielfach Holzfässer eine große Rolle. Einmal große, fest im Keller installierte, mit 3.000 oder 5.000 Litern Inhalt, manchmal auch mehr. Seltener findet auch die Gärung von Weiß- oder Roséweinen in solchen Fässern statt. Häufiger schon die zweite, die malolaktische oder Milchsäuregärung, bei der Apfelsäure, deren Geschmack wir als „grün" oder „grasig" empfinden, in mildere Milchsäure abgebaut wird, wobei auch Kohlensäure entsteht, die manchmal mit den Weinen in die Flasche kommt und sie leicht „bitzeln" läßt. Wesentlich beim Faßausbau ist die „Atmung", bei der der Wein mit Sauerstoff in homöopathischen Dosen in Berührung kommt. Das hat zur Folge, daß sich Farb- und Geschmacksstoffe verändern und neu bilden. Komplexe mikrochemische und -biologische Vorgänge laufen ab, bei denen sich aus den Primäraromen der Trauben

die Sekundären Geschmacksnoten bilden, die wir an großen Weinen schätzen, jene subtilen Düfte, die von Kennern zum Beispiel als Tabak, Waldbeeren, Trüffel identifiziert werden (um nur einige der bei Rotweinen meist genannten zu erwähnen).

Für die großen Weine (und nur die) des Bordelais spielt die Barrique eine herausragende Rolle, jenes 225 Liter aufnehmende Faß aus Eichenholz. Es ist so klein, weil es vor Jahrhunderten als Transportfaß in Gebrauch kam und eine Größe hat, daß es sich ohne großes Hebegerät auf Segelschiffe verladen ließ. Heute ist der Umgang mit der Barrique eine Wissenschaft. Es kommt Eichenholz unterschiedlicher Art und Herkunft zum Einsatz. Auch die „Röstung" spielt eine Rolle - die Faßdauben werden mit Hilfe von Feuer an der Innenseite und Wasser von außen in Form gebracht. Dabei werden sie innen mehr oder weniger angekohlt. Neues Eichenholz gibt ein Vanilleähnliches Aroma an den Inhalt ab, das sich vor allem bei Weißwein bemerkbar macht und den Charakter großer Weißer aus Burgund oder Kalifornien wesentlich mitbestimmt. Diese Weine werden zum Teil in neuen Eichenfässern vergoren.

Die großen Roten von Bordeaux (wie jene von Kalifornien, die auf die gleiche Art ausgebaut werden) reifen nach der Gärung zwei Jahre in Barriques und ein Jahr in der Flasche, ehe sie an den Handel geliefert werden. Alle drei bis vier Monate findet ein „Abstich" statt, bei der der Wein von den Trubstoffen abgezogen wird, die auf den Boden des Fasses gesunken sind (dessen Form begünstigt dieses Verfahren). Dabei kommen neue Fässer zum Einsatz wie auch solche, die schon für ein oder zwei Jahrgänge gebraucht wurden. Je älter ein Faß wird, um so weniger des geschätzten vanilleartigen Eichentones gibt es an den Wein ab. Meist wird eine Mischung aus neuen und gebrauchten Fässern eingesetzt. Vor der Abfüllung verkostet man den Inhalt jedes Fasses und entscheidet, ob die Qualität für den „Grand Vin" reicht oder nur für den preiswerteren „Zweitwein", der einen anderen Namen trägt. Der Anteil an neuen Barriques im Keller ist ein wesentlicher Kostenfaktor beim Ausbau eines Weins. Eine neue Barrique kostet, je nach Hersteller und Holzart, zwischen 1000 und 1500 Mark. (Gebrauchte Fässer der großen Häuser werden von minder klassifizierten Gütern gekauft und benutzt, etwa für die Crus bourgeois). Für die Abfüllung wird der Wein aus den Barriques wieder in einem großen Faß oder Tank vereint, damit alle Flaschen die gleiche Qualität enthalten.

Das gepflegte Barriquelager ist ein Prestige-Objekt, das jedes Weingut gerne vorzeigt, im Prospekt abbildet oder gar auf die Etiketten druckt. Es ist zugleich ein Bekenntnis zur lebendigen Tradition wie zum Fortschritt und dokumentiert den hohen Qualitätsanspruch eines Hauses.

Ein Château erster Kategorie verfügt in der Regel über ein Erstjahres- und ein Zweitjahres-Chai sowie einen Flaschenkeller. Im Bordelais ist das Chai öfter eine Halle zu ebener Erde als ein Keller. Günstig ist es, wenn das Zweitjahres-Chai unter dem für den neuen Wein liegt, so daß das Umfüllen durch Schwerkraft erfolgen kann. Das ideale Klima für die Reifung von Wein im Faß ist bei einer Temperatur von 10 bis 14 °C und einer relativen Luftfeuchtigkeit von 70% Prozent. Anders als beim Flaschenlager ist eine gewisse jahreszeitliche Schwankung der Temperatur erwünscht; sie begünstigt das Klären des Weins durch Absetzen der Trubstoffe.

Um einen großen Wein zu machen, braucht es einen Weinberg mit geeignetem Boden und möglichst idealem Klima; Menschen mit einer Leidenschaft für Qualität. Und natürlich die entsprechenden Mittel. Daß die Häuser, in denen große Weine entstehen, diesen Anspruch auch nach außen dokumentieren, ist einer der Faktoren, der das Reisen in Weinbaugebieten zum Erlebnis macht.

The Art of Winemaking

Peter C. Hubschmid

Moses Wrote the First Wine Law

The clay tablets of Hammurabi, who founded the Kingdom of Babylon in 1800 BC, mention wine being sold in specialised shops. The Law of Moses contains detailed instructions on the cultivation of grapes and wine making. As far as the hygienic aspect of wine preparation is concerned, these instructions are exemplary and to this day still constitute the basis of pressing and cultivating kosher wine.

Wine was held in high steem by the Greeks and the Romans. The amphorae in which it was transported were found along the ancient shipping routes on the bed of the Mediterranean. In his work "Natural History", Pliny the Elder dealt with the subject of wine growing in great detail, based on personal observation as well as by reverting to the works of Varros, who himself had been educated by the Carthaginian Mago.

Quality was important even then: in his book on agriculture, Cato the Elder wrote that grapes should not be harvested before they are fully ripe so as not to destroy the good reputation of the wine pressed from the grapes. In addition, he urged that cleanliness be observed to prevent the wine from turning into vinegar.

Pliny described a new type of "Greek press"; this imposing winepress generated pressure by means of a tree trunk, acting as a lever, and an immense stone weight suspended from a spindle. To this day its gentle effect on the pressed grapes remains unsurpassed.

According to our knowledge of Greek and Roman wine, it would hardly taste good to those of us who appreciate the smooth, full-bodied Cabernet, delicate Riesling and fruity Chardonnay. Their "noble" wines were oxidized, with all kinds of spices and preservatives added, and could only be drunk when diluted with water.

The spaciously laid-out villa, the estate of the Romans, is the oldest example known to us of a type of building created for the purpose of producing wine (alongside other agricultural produce). The courtyard surrounded by living and working quarters formed the centre of rural life. At harvest time the carts would be unloaded here and the grapes brought to the press. Amphorae served as containers for the wine. Barrels were not common in Rome until the 3rd Century AD.

The Basic Rules for Great Wines

In the middle ages wine was developed primarily by the monasteries; the Burgundian Benedictines in Cluny and the Cistercians in Eberbach on the banks of the Rhine. The monks researched and improved the cultivation of vines and cellaring, thereby laying the foundations of modern wine growing.

The term "wine making" is of American origin and means the processing of the grapes up to the bottling of the wine. In the New World (in wine terms, this includes Australia, New Zealand and South Africa as well as the Americas) the attitude towards wine making is pragmatic, vinification and maturing of the wines the best wine. In Europe, on the other hand, tradition mainly dictates which varieties are planted and how the wines are cultivated.

The basic rules are, however, the same everywhere: good, all the more great wines orginate in the vineyard. The birth of a great wine begins with the planting of a vine in a spot which can offer the best conditions for the variety of grape in question. This would include: the composition of the soil and supply of water; the total number of sunshine hours per year; the difference in temperature between day and night and summer and winter; the breeze that blows away the mist or even the mists themselves that – in the Sauternes region – stimulate the development of noble rot on the grapes that makes the wine so unique and precious. And in Germany severe frost could even be required if "Eiswein" (ice wine) is to be produced, which is pressed from frozen grapes. On the Moselle and the Rhine as well as in Burgundy the sunniest slopes are deemed the best, but in Cassis on the French Riviera the finest whites thrive on the north slopes, just as Mago the Carthaginian recommended for his North African homeland.

The roots of a vine can only absorb a certain amount of minerals from the soil to transport to the fruit. It is these minerals that determine the character of a wine. Very old vines produce only a few grapes, albeit with a very intense taste. Nowadays, to obtain the same effect with newly estab-lished vineyards, more vines are planted per hectare. In addition, the vines are pruned in the winter before any new growth appears so that each one bears only a little fruit. In this way, there are more roots per grape, therefore producing an intensity of taste that was previously only found in vin-tages from very old vines. In wine terms, less is more. If one can be satisfied with a small yield, that is, less wine per hectare, the wine produced has more dry extract and thus more character and taste.

The Vine as Creator of the Cultural Landscape

Alongside olive trees and grain, the vine was one of the first cultural plants to determine the landscape. For producing the best wine possible from healthy, ripe grapes the winery must be close to the vineyards, so that the fruit arrives intact and fresh at the press. The ideal location for produc-ing great wines is a winery in the middle of the vineyards – a picture that occurs on labels from all over the world.

The facilities for pressing the wine should be sufficiently large to cope with the year's vintage within a few weeks. If the grapes have reached optimum ripeness, only a few days remain to harvest them in this state. The pressing facilities represent one of the most expensive investments on a wine estate and for at least eleven months of the year they stand idle.

Today stainless steel is the material of choice for delivery stations, destemmers, presses, pumps, pipes and tanks. Its cool, matt-finished aesthetic dictates the appearance of a modern winery. It is easy to keep clean and facilitates the observance of hygiene standards. Also, it does not cause a reaction or combination with the wine, nor in particular with the acid it contains. Inox tanks allow temperature control, which is necessary for performing optimum fermentation; mostly the temperature has to be cooled down but also, less commonly, raised.

In order to make the most of the vintage, not only the grapes but also the must and wine should be treated with as much care as possible. Allowing the liquid to flow is better than pumping it. If possible, therefore, wineries are laid out in such as way that gravity takes care of the transport from one station to the next. Often only – the "tête de cuvée"is used for the best wines that flows out of the must by its own weight alone, that is without pressing. Selective harvesting and processing of the grapes is important for a perfect result. Each grape should be harvested in a state of optimum ripeness; some varieties ripen early, others late. In addition there are regional differences. The cuvée, the blending of the varieties, does not take place until fermentation is complete.

Barrels Determine the Layout of the Cellar

Wooden barrels frequently play a large role in the maturation (i.e., cellar ageing) of the young wine prior to bottling; large wooden barrels, permanently installed in the cellar, with a capacity of 3.000 or 5.000 litres, sometimes more. White or rosé wine is sometimes fermented in barrels such as these, though less commonly; more frequent is the second malolactic or lactic acid fermentation process. Here, the malic acid, which tastes "green" or "grassy" to us, is broken down into milder lactic acid; during this process carbonic dioxide is also produced, which is sometimes transferred to the bottle with the wines, giving them a light sparkle. Air plays an important part during the ageing of a wine in wood – oxygen in minute quantities diffusing through the wood helps the wine mature. The result is that colourings and flavourings undergo a change and re-form; also, complex microchemical and microbiological processes take place through which the secondary taste characteristics are created from the primary aroma of the grapes. This is what we appreciate in great wines, the subtle notes that can be identified by experts as tobacco, forest berries or truffles (to mention but a few of the descriptions most commonly applied to red wine).

With respect to the great wines (and only these) of Bordeaux, the barrique plays an outstanding role – an oak barrel with a 225-litre capacity. Its small size is due to the fact that it came into use centuries ago as a transport barrel, its size allowing it to be loaded onto sailing ships without the use of heavy loading gear. Today, the use of the barrique is a science in itself. Different types of oak of different origin are used. The "toasting" also plays a role – with the aid of fire on the inside and water on the outside the staves of the barrel are formed. In this way they are more or less "charred" on the inside. New oak produces a vanilla-type aroma, noticeable above all in white wine and in its determining influence on the character of great wines from Burgundy or California. These wines are sometimes fermented in new oak barrels.

After fermentation, the great reds of Bordeaux (like those of California that are cultivated in the same way) mature for two years in barriques and age for one year in bottles before being delivered onto the market. Every three to four months the wine is "racked", that is drawn off from the lees that have sunk to the bottom of the barrel (conveniently shaped for this process). New barrels are then used as well as barrels that have already been used for one or two vintages. The older a barrel gets, the less the wine takes on the vanilla-type oak character. A mixture of new and used barriques is mostly used. Before bottling the wine, the contents of each barrel are tasted and it is decided whether the quality is sufficient for the "grand vin" or simply for a less expensive "second wine", which goes by a different name. The proportion of new barriques in the cellar is an important cost factor maturing wines. Depending in each case on the manufacturer and type of wood, a new barrique costs between $ 350 and $ 550. (Used barrels are bought from the great estates to be used by estates of a lower category, for example for the crus bourgeois.) At the bottling stage, the wine from the barriques is again combined in a large barrel or tank so that all of the bottles contain wine of the same quality.

The well-kept stock of barriques is a prestige object that any wine estate likes to show off; pictures of it appear in advertising and labels. It is at once a declaration of a living tradition and of progress and documents the high demand for quality of a particular estate.

As a general rule, a chateau of the highest category has a chai for the first year and one for the second year as well as a bottle cellar. In Bordeaux the chai is more often a hall on level ground than a cellar. It is advantageous if the chai for the second year is situated below the one for the new wine because the transfer of the wine can then take place by the force of gravity. The ideal climate for wine to mature in barrels is a temperature of between 10°C and 14°C and a relative humidity of seventy percent. Certain seasonal fluctuations in the temperature are desirable, though a constant temperature is optimum once the bottles are stored. These fluctuations in temperature have a beneficial effect on clearing the wine by removing the lees.

To produce a great wine requires a vineyard with suitable soil and a climate as near to ideal as possible; also, people with a passion for quality and, of course, the appropriate means. The fact that the estates in which great wines are produced also outwardly document these demands is one of the factors that makes travelling into wine-growing regions such an adventure.

L'art du vigneron

Peter C. Hubschmid

Moïse et la première loi du vin

Déjà sur les plaquettes d'argile d'Hammourabi, qui a créé le royaume de Babylone vers 1800 avant Jésus-Christ, le négoce du vin est décrit comme un commerce particulier. Dans les lois de Moïse, on trouve également des réglementations précises concernant la culture de la vigne et la production du vin. Elles prônent des mesures d'hygiène qui sont exemplaires et servent encore de fondement pour le pressurage et la production du vin casher.

Chez les Grecs et les Romains, le vin avait une signification très importante et on retrouve les amphores dans lesquelles il était transporté sur le fond de la mer Méditerranée tout au long des routes maritimes de l'Antiquité. Pline l'Ancien s'est intéressé longuement à la vigne dans son "Histoire naturelle", rédigée à partir de ses observations personnelles, mais aussi avec des emprunts aux écrits de Varron, qui l'avait lui-même appris de Magon le carthaginois.

Déjà à cette époque, on se préoccupait de qualité: Caton l'Ancien précise dans son livre sur l'agriculture que le raisin doit être ramassé à point pour que le vin qui en est tiré ne perde pas sa bonne réputation. Il recommande aussi une hygiène stricte pour que le vin ne se transforme pas en vinaigre.

Pline le Jeune décrit comme une "presse grecque" innovante une imposante machine, composée d'un tronc d'arbre servant de levier et d'un énorme poids en pierre suspendu à un axe vertical. Sa pression douce sur les grappes n'a encore jamais été égalée.

D'après ce que nous savons des vins des Grecs et des Romains, nous, qui apprécions les cabernets qui ont du corps, les riesling et les chardonnays fruités, ne devrions guère nous en régaler. Ils étaient oxydés avec toutes sortes d'épices et d'additifs destinés à la conservation, et on ne pouvait les apprécier que lorsqu'ils étaient dilués avec de l'eau.

La "villa" – domaine de campagne des Romains – est le plus ancien exemple que nous connaissions d'un type de bâtiment réservé à la production du vin et des autres fruit de la terre. La cour, entourée de constructions destinées à l'habitat et à l'agriculture, constituait le centre de la vie rurale. Pendant la saison des récoltes, on déchargeait là les charrettes qui apportaient le raisin au pressoir. Le vin était conservé dans des amphores, les tonneaux ne s'étant généralisés à Rome qu'au 3ème siècle de notre ère.

Les règles de base pour les grands vins

Au Moyen âge, c'est essentiellement dans les monastères – chez les bénédictins bourguignons de Cluny ou les cisterciens d'Eberbach-in-Rheingau – que la viticulture a continué de se développer. Les moines ont fait des recherches et amélioré la plantation des ceps ainsi que les techniques de pressurage, créant ainsi les fondements de la viticulture et de l'œnologie modernes.

La fabrication du vin englobe au sens strict le traitement du raisin jusqu'au remplissage des bouteilles. Dans le Nouveau Monde – en ce qui concerne le vin, l'Amérique, l'Australie, la Nouvelle-Zélande et l'Afrique du Sud en font partie – l'attitude vis-à-vis de la production du vin est marquée par le pragmatisme, selon le principe: Comment pouvons-nous faire le meilleur vin? En Europe, en revanche, c'est essentiellement en fonction de la tradition que l'on choisit les cépages et les processus de vinification.

Les principes de base sont cependant partout les mêmes: les bons, et à fortiori les grands vins, sont créés avant tout dans les vignes. La naissance d'un grand vin commence avec la plantation des pieds à un endroit qui offre à chaque cépage les meilleures conditions de développement: composition du sol et pluviosité; somme des heures d'ensoleillement annuel; différence de température entre le jour et la nuit, entre l'été et l'hiver; brise fréquente, qui chasse le brouillard, ou au contraire présence d'un brouillard qui, comme dans la région de Sauternes, s'élève en apportant au raisin la pourriture noble qui rend les vins de ces domaines uniques et précieux. Même un gel sévère est parfois recherché, comme en Allemagne où l'on fabrique du vin de glace en pressant du raisin gelé. S'il est vrai que dans les vallées de la Moselle et du Rhin, comme en Bourgogne, les coteaux ensoleillés sont les meilleurs, les vins blancs les plus fins de Cassis ou de la Côte d'Azur se développent sur les coteaux orientés au nord. Magon de Carthage recommandait déjà cette disposition pour sa patrie nord-africaine.

Avec ses racines, un cep de vigne ne peut retirer du sol et transmettre aux fruits qu'une quantité déterminée de sels minéraux. Ce sont eux qui influencent le caractère du vin. Les très vieux ceps produisent peu de grappes, mais leur raisin a un goût très intense. Pour obtenir le même effet avec des vignobles récents, on plante davantage de pieds par hectare et on taille les ceps assez courts en hiver pour que chacun ne puisse porter que peu de grappes. On obtient ainsi plus de racines par grappe et une intensité de goût réservée jusque là à la récolte des très vieux vignobles. En ce qui concerne le vin, "le moins, c'est le plus". Si on se contente d'une récolte plus faible, produisant moins d'hectolitres par hectare, on obtient du vin dont l'extrait sec est supérieur, c'est à dire du vin avec plus de caractère et plus de goût.

La vigne, créatrice du paysage

La vigne est avec l'olivier et les céréales une des cultures primitives qui ont déterminé le paysage. Pour obtenir le meilleur vin possible à partir de raisins sains et mûrs, il faut transformer des grappes intactes et fraîchement cueillies. Le pressurage doit donc se faire près des vignobles. La situation du domaine et du pressoir au milieu des vignes est donc depuis des siècles la condition idéale pour la production d'un grand vin, et cette image est reproduite dans le monde entier sous des formes variées, grâce aux étiquettes collées sur les bouteilles.

Lorsque les raisins ont obtenu la maturité optimale, il ne reste que quelques jours pour les récolter. Les installations pour le pressurage doivent donc être assez grandes pour venir à bout de la récolte d'une année en quelques semaines. Ces installations font partie des investissements les plus coûteux pour un domaine viticole, et elles sont en sommeil pendant au moins onze mois de l'année.

Pour la réception, le foulage et le pressurage, la pompe, les tuyaux et les citernes, l'acier inoxydable est aujourd'hui le matériau de prédilection. Son esthétique froide et brillante détermine l'image des pressoirs modernes. Il facilite le nettoyage et le respect des normes d'hygiène. Il n'entre en réaction chimique ni avec le vin, ni avec les acides qui s'y trouvent. Les citernes en acier inoxydable facilitent aussi le réglage de la température, si important pour la fermentation: il faut en général rafraîchir, parfois aussi réchauffer.

Pour obtenir la meilleure qualité à partir de la récolte, il faut traiter les raisins, mais aussi le moût et le vin, avec autant de ménagement que possible: il vaut mieux laisser couler que pomper. C'est pour cela que les installations de pressurage sont souvent disposées de manière à permettre l'écoulement par gravité d'une station à l'autre. Pour les meilleurs vins, on n'utilise souvent que la "tête de cuvée" qui sort sans pressurage sous l'effet de son propre poids. Pour ce résultat optimal, une récolte et une fabrication sélectives sont essentielles: chaque grappe doit être ramassée à maturité. Certains cépages mûrissent tôt, d'autres plus tard, et il y a des différences selon les orientations. La "cuvée", c'est-à-dire le mélange des cépages, n'est réalisée qu'après la fermentation.

Le tonneau, mesure du pressoir

Pour la maturation du jeune vin avant la mise en bouteille, les tonneaux en bois jouent souvent un rôle important. Certains, fixés dans les caves, peuvent contenir 3 000 voire 5 000 litres, parfois plus. La fermentation des vins blancs et rosés a rarement lieu dans ces foudres. On emploie plutôt la fermentation lactique, dans laquelle l'acide malique – dont nous trouvons le goût "vert" ou "herbeux" – est transformé en acide lactique plus doux. L'acide carbonique ainsi créé entre parfois avec le vin dans les bouteilles et le fait légèrement pétiller. Pendant la phase de maturation en tonneau, la "respiration" – au cours de laquelle le vin entre en contact à dose homéopathique avec l'oxygène – est fondamentale. Elle entraîne la transformation des substances qui donnent au vin sa couleur et son goût, ainsi que la mise en œuvre de phénomènes microchimiques et biologiques complexes, au cours desquels le goût primaire du raisin se transforme en cet arôme secondaire que nous apprécions dans les grands vins. Parmi les parfums subtils identifiés par les connaisseurs, "tabac", "fruits des bois" et "truffe" sont les plus souvent cités pour les vins rouges.

Pour les grands vins du Bordelais – et seulement pour ceux-là –, la "barrique", un tonneau en chêne de 225 litres, joue un rôle essentiel. S'il est si petit, c'est parce qu'il servait il y a plusieurs siècles au transport du vin, et devait pouvoir être chargé sans moyen de levage sur les voiliers. Aujourd'hui, la fabrication de la barrique est devenue une science. On utilise du chêne de plusieurs espèces et de différentes provenances. Les douves du tonneau sont mises en forme avec l'aide de feu à l'intérieur et d'eau à l'extérieur, opération au cours de laquelle la face interne est plus ou moins carbonisée. Le chêne fraîchement coupé donne au contenu un arôme de vanille, particulièrement sensible dans les vins blancs. Il influence le caractère des grands vins de Bourgogne et de Californie qui fermentent partiellement dans des tonneaux neufs en chêne.

Après la fermentation, les grands Bordeaux rouges – comme les vins rouges de Californie, produits selon une méthode semblable – sont conservés deux ans dans des barriques, puis un an en bouteille, avant d'être commercialisés. La forme du tonneau favorise la séparation entre le vin et les lies qui se déposent sur le fond et sont éliminées tous les trois ou quatre mois grâce à un soutirage. On utilise alors des tonneaux neufs et d'autres qui ont déjà servi pour une ou deux récoltes. Plus le tonneau est vieux, moins il donne au vin cet arôme de vanille très apprécié qui vient du bois de chêne. On emploie donc le plus souvent un mélange de barriques neuves et anciennes. Avant la mise en bouteilles, on goûte le contenu de chaque tonneau et on décide si la qualité est suffisante pour un "grand cru" ou si elle convient seulement à un vin de deuxième catégorie, meilleur marché, qui porte un nom différent. La proportion de barriques neuves dans une cave est un facteur financier très important dans la production d'un vin. Une barrique neuve coûte, en fonction de l'essence et du fabricant, entre 3 500 et 5 000 francs. Les tonneaux d'occasion des grands domaines sont rachetés par des viticulteurs moins bien classés et utilisés pour les "crus bourgeois". Avant l'embouteillage, le vin de toutes les barriques est versé dans une grande cuve ou une citerne afin que toutes les bouteilles possèdent la même qualité.

Un chai bien entretenu est un objet de prestige que chaque domaine montre volontiers et présente dans ses prospectus ou même sur ses étiquettes. Ce signe, qui montre à la fois l'appartenance à une tradition vivante et la reconnaissance du progrès, confirme les hautes exigences de qualité d'un domaine.

Un Château de première catégorie dispose en général d'un "chai d'un an" et d'un "chai de deux ans", ainsi que d'un cellier pour les bouteilles. Dans le Bordelais, le chai est souvent un grand espace à rez-de-chaussée qui ressemble à une cave. Lorsque le chai de deux ans est disposé sous celui où se trouve le vin de l'année, la position est particulièrement favorable pour que le remplissage se fasse par gravité. La température idéale pour la maturation du vin en tonneau varie entre 10 et 14 degrés, avec un taux d'humidité relatif de 70%. Contrairement à ce qui se passe dans les celliers où reposent les bouteilles, des différences de températures au gré des saisons sont souhaitées, car elles favorisent le dépôt des lies et donc la clarification du vin.

Pour créer un grand vin, on a besoin: d'un vignoble avec un sol adapté, d'un climat idéal, d'hommes et de femmes animés d'une passion pour la qualité, et naturellement des moyens correspondants. Que les domaines où naissent les grands vins veuillent présenter ces critères de qualité au public est un des facteurs qui transforment un voyage dans une région viticole en aventure.

Addresses

Château d'Arsac
33460 Margaux
Tel   +33-5 56 58 83 90
Fax   +33-5 56 58 83 08

Visits with prior booking only

Architect: Patrick Hernandez

Wines:
Chateau Le Monteil d'Arsac,
Ruban bleu du Chateau d'Arsac

Château Branaire
33250 Saint-Julien
Tel   +33-5 56 59 25 86
Fax   +33-5 56 59 16 26
e-mail branaire@branaire.com

Opening hours:
9.00-12.00 and 14.00-16.00
Visits with prior booking only

Architects:
Bernard, Marcel and
Jean-Marie Mazieres

Wines:
Le Château Branaire (Grand Cru
Classé - Saint-Julien),
Le Château Duluc (Appelation
Saint-Julien)

Château Cos d'Estournel
33180 Saint-Estèphe
Tel   +33-5 56 73 15 50
Fax   +33-5 56 59 72 59
e-mail estournel@estournel.com

Opening hours:
9.30-12.30 and 14.00-18.00.
Visits with prior booking only
(48 hours in advance)

Wines:
Cos d'Estournel (s'Estèphe AOC);
Les Pagodes de Cos (S'Estephe
AOC)

Adressen

Château d'Arsac
33460 Margaux
Tel   +33-5 56 58 83 90
Fax   +33-5 56 58 83 08

Besichtigung nach Voranmeldung

Architekt:
Patrick Hernandez

Weine:
Château Le Monteil d'Arsac,
Ruban bleu du Château d'Arsac

Château Branaire
33250 Saint-Julien
Tel   +33-5 56 59 25 86
Fax   +33-5 56 59 16 26
e-mail branaire@branaire.com

Öffnungszeiten:
9.00 bis 12.00 und
14.00 bis 16.00 Uhr
Besichtigung nach Voranmeldung

Architekten:
Bernard, Marcel und
Jean-Marie Mazieres

Weine:
Le Château Branaire (Grand Cru
Classé - Saint-Julien),
Le Château Duluc (Appelation
Saint-Julien)

Château Cos d'Estournel
33180 Saint-Estèphe
Tel   +33-5 56 73 15 50
Fax   +33-5 56 59 72 59
e-mail estournel@estournel.com

Öffnungszeiten: 9.30 bis 12.30
und 14.00 bis 18.00 Uhr
Besichtigung nach Voranmeldung
(48 Stunden vorher)

Weine: Cos d'Estournel (s'Estèphe
AOC); Les Pagodes de Cos
(S'Estephe AOC)

Adresses

Château d'Arsac
33460 Margaux
Tel   +33-05 56 58 83 90
Fax   +33-05 56 58 83 08

Visites sur rendez-vous

Architecte: Patrick Hernandez

Vins:
Château Le Monteil d'Arsac,
Ruban bleu du Château d'Arsac

Château Branaire
33250 Saint-Julien
Tel   +33-05 56 59 25 86
Fax   +33-05 56 59 16 26
e-mail branaire@branaire.com

Heures d'ouverture:
de 9h00 à 12h00 et
de 14h00 à 16h00
Visites sur rendez-vous

Architectes:
Bernard, Marcel et
Jean-Marie Mazieres

Vins:
Le Château Branaire (Grand Cru
classé – Saint-Julien),
Le Château Duluc (Appellation
Saint-Julien)

Château Cos d'Estournel
33180 Saint-Estèphe
Tel   +33-05 56 73 15 50
Fax   +33-05 56 59 72 59
e-mail estournel@estournel.com

Heures d'ouverture:
9h30 à 12h30 et 14h00 à 18h00
Visite sur rendez-vous
(48 heures à l'avance)

Vins:
Cos d'Estournel (Saint-Estèphe
AOC); Les Pagodes de Cos
(Saint-Estèphe AOC)

Domaines Henry Martin
33250 Saint-Julien Beychevelle
Tel   +33-5 56 59 08 18
Fax   +33-5 56 59 16 18

Öffnungszeiten:
Montag bis Donnerstag: 8.00 bis
12.30 und 14.00 bis 18.00 Uhr
Freitag: 8.00 bis 12.00 und
14.00 bis 17.00 Uhr

Besichtigung nach Voranmeldung

Architekt: Alain Triaud

Weine:
Château Gloria (65% Cabernet
Sauvignon, 25% Merlot, 5%
Cabernet Franc, 5% Petit
Verdot), Château Saint-Pierre
(75% Cabernet Sauvignon, 10%
Cabernet Franc, 15% Merlot),
Château Bel Air (65% Cabernet
Sauvignon, 35% Merlot)

Château Lafite-Rothschild
33250 Pauillac
Tel   +33-5 56 73 18 18
Fax   +33-5 56 59 26 83

Öffnungszeiten:
Mo-Do von 9.00 bis 11.00 und
von 13.30. bis 15.30 Uhr
Fr von 9.00 bis 11.00 und von
13.30. bis 14.30 Uhr

Besichtigung nach Voranmeldung: geführte Touren

Architekt: u.a. Ricardo Bofill

Weine:
Carruades de Lafite (grand vin),
Carruades de Lafite (second vin)

Händler Deutschland:
HAWESKO GmbH, Tornesch;
Segnitz & Co GmbH, Bremen

Händler USA:
Seagram Chateau & Estate
Wines, New York; Pasternak,
Greenwich

Domaines Henry Martin
33250 Saint-Julien Beychevelle
Tel   +33-5 56 59 08 18
Fax   +33-5 56 59 16 18

Opening hours:
monday until thursday:
8.00-12.30 and 14.00-18.00
friday: 8.00-12.00 and
14.00-17.00

Visits with prior booking only

Architect: Alain Triaud

Wines:
Château Gloria (65% Cabernet
Sauvignon, 25% Merlot, 5%
Cabernet Franc, 5% Petit
Verdot), Château Saint-Pierre
(75% Cabernet Sauvignon, 10%
Cabernet Franc, 15% Merlot),
Château Bel Air (65% Cabernet
Sauvignon, 35% Merlot)

Château Lafite-Rothschild
33250 Pauillac
Tel   +33-5 56 73 18 18
Fax   +33-5 56 59 26 83

Opening hours:
Mon-Thurs from 9.00-11.00
and 13.30-15.30
Frid from 9.00-11.00 and
13.30-14.30

Visits only with prior booking:
organised tours

Architect:
Ricardo Bofill and others

Wines:
Carruades de Lafite (grand vin),
Carruades de Lafite (second vin)

Wine merchants Germany:
HAWESKO GmbH, Tornesch;
Segnitz & Co GmbH, Bremen

Wine merchants USA:
Seagram Chateau & Estate
Wines, New York; Pasternak,
Greenwich

Domaines Henry Martin
33250 Saint-Julien Beychevelle
Tel   +33-05 56 59 08 18
Fax   +33-05 56 59 16 18

Heures d'ouverture:
lundi au jeudi: de 8h00 à 12h30
et 14h00 à 18h00
vendredi: de 8h00 à 12h00 et
14h00 à 17h00

Visites sur rendez-vous

Architecte: Alain Triaud

Wines:
Château Gloria (65% cabernet
sauvignon, 25% merlot, 5%
cabernet franc, 5% petit verdot),
Château Saint-Pierre (75%
cabernet sauvignon, 10% cabernet franc, 15% merlot), Château
Bel Air (65% cabernet sauvignon, 35% merlot)

Château Lafite-Rothschild
33250 Pauillac
Tel   +33-05 56 73 18 18
Fax   +33-05 56 59 26 83

Heures d'ouverture:
du lundi au jeudi de 9h00 à
11h00 et de 13h30 à 15h30
le vendredi de 9h00 à 11h00 et
de 13h30 à 14h30

Visites guidées sur rendez-vous

Architecte:
Ricardo Bofill, entre autres

Vins:
Carruades de Lafite (grand vin),
Carruades de Lafite (second vin)

Négociants en Allemagne:
Hanseatisches Wein- und
Sektkontor (HAWESKO),
Hambourg; Segnitz & Co GmbH,
Brème

Négociants aux Etats-Unis:
Seagram Chateau & Estate
Wines, New York; Pasternak,
Greenwich

Château Léoville Poyferré
33250 Saint-Julien
Beychevelle
Tel   +33-05 56-59 08 30
Fax +33-05 56-59 60 09

Visites du lundi au vendredi sur
rendez-vous

Architecte: Olivier Brochet

Vins:
Château Léoville-Poyferré (Cru
classé, Saint-Julien), Château
Moulin Riche (Cru Bourgeois,
Saint-Julien), Marques: Pavillon
des Connétables (Autre cru,
Saint-Julien)

Château Lynch-Bages
33180 Pauillac
Tel   +33-05 56 73 24 00
Fax +33-05 56 59 26 42

Heures d'ouverture:
de 9h00 à 12h00 et
de 14h00 à 18h00

Visites guidées exclusivement

Architectes:
Patric Dillon, Jean de Gastines

Vins:
Château Lynch-Bages, Château
Haut-Bages Averous, M Lynch:
Blanc de Lynch-Bages

Château Pichon-Longueville
Saint-Lambert
33180 Pauillac
Tel   +33-05 56 73 17 17
Fax +33-05 56 73 17 28

Heures d'ouverture:
de 9h00 à 12h00 et
de 14h00 à 18h00

Visites guidées exclusivement

Architectes:
Patric Dillon, Jean de Gastines

Vins:
Château Pichon-Longueville,
Les Tourelles de Longueville

Château Léoville Poyferré
33250 Saint-Julien
Beychevelle
Tel   +33-5 56 59 08 30
Fax +33-5 56 59 60 09

Besichtigung Montag bis Freitag
nach Vereinbarung

Architekt: Olivier Brochet

Weine:
Château Léoville-Poyferré (Cru
classé, Saint-Julien), Château
Moulin Riche (Cru Bourgeois,
Saint-Julien), Marques: Pavillon
des Connétables (Autre cru,
Saint-Julien)

Château Lynch-Bages
33180 Pauillac
Tel   +33-5 56 73 24 00
Fax +33-5 56 59 26 42

Öffnungszeiten:
9.00 bis 12.00 Uhr und
14.00 bis 18.00 Uhr

nur geführte Besichtigung

Architekten: Patric Dillon, Jean de
Gastines

Weine: Château Lynch-Bages,
Château Haut-Bages Averous, M.
Lynch: Blanc de Lynch-Bages

Château Pichon-Longueville
Saint-Lambert
33180 Pauillac
Tel   +33-5 56 73 17 17
Fax +33-5 56 73 17 28

Öffnungszeiten:
9.00 bis 12.00 Uhr und
14.00 bis 18.00 Uhr

nur geführte Besichtigung

Architekten:
Patric Dillon, Jean de Gastines

Weine:
Château Pichon-Longueville,
Les Tourelles de Longueville

Château Léoville Poyferré
33250 Saint-Julien
Beychevelle
Tel   +33-5 56 59 08 30
Fax +33-5 56 59 60 09

Visits Mon to Frid, prior booking
necessary

Architect: Olivier Brochet

Wines:
Château Léoville-Poyferré (Cru
classé, Saint-Julien), Château
Moulin Riche (Cru Bourgeois,
Saint-Julien), Marques: Pavillon
des Connétables (Autre cru,
Saint-Julien)

Château Lynch-Bages
33180 Pauillac
Tel   +33-5 56 73 24 00
Fax +33-5 56 59 26 42

Opening hours:
9.00-12.00 and 14.00-18.00

organised tours only

Architects:
Patric Dillon, Jean de Gastines

Wines:
Château Lynch-Bages, Château
Haut-Bages Averous, M Lynch:
Blanc de Lynch-Bages

Château Pichon-Longueville
Saint-Lambert
33180 Pauillac
Tel   +33-5 56 73 17 17
Fax +33-5 56 73 17 28

Opening hours:
9.00-12.00 and 14.00-18.00

organised tours only

Architects:
Patric Dillon, Jean de Gastines

Wines:
Château Pichon-Longueville,
Les Tourelles de Longueville

Artesa (früher Codorniu Napa)
1345 Henry Road
Napa, CA 94559
Tel +1-707-224 16 68
Fax +1-707-224 16 72

Öffnungszeiten:
täglich 10.00 bis 17.00 Uhr

Führungen:
11.00 und 14.00 Uhr
(oder nach Vereinbarung)

Architekt:
Domingo Triary, E. R. Bouligny

Weine:
Codorniu Napa methode champenoise sparkling wines, Artesa Chardonnay, Pinot Noir

Beringer Vineyards
2000 Main Street
St. Helena, CA 94574
Tel +1-707-963 71 15
Fax +1-707-963 17 35
e-mail info@bwecorp.com

Öffnungszeiten:
täglich 9.30 bis 18.00 (Mai bis Okt.); 9.30 bis 17.00 Uhr (Nov. bis April)

Führungen jede halbe Stunde
(keine Voranmeldung möglich)

Architekt: u.a. A. Schroepfer

Weine:
Private Reserve Napa Valley Cabernet Sauvignon, Private Reserve Napa Valley Chardonnay, Napa Valley Howell Mountain Merlot, Bancroft Ranch, Napa Valley Cabernet Sauvignon, Napa Valley Chardonnay, Napa Valley Fume' Blanc, Knights Valley Alluvium (proprietary blend), Knights Valley Alluvium Blanc (proprietary blend), North Coast Zinfandel, North Coast Pinot Noir, California Zinfandel Blush, California Collection Sauvignon Blanc, Chardonnay, Merlot and Cabernet Sauvignon

Händler Deutschland:
Reidelmeister & Ulrichs GmbH, Bremen

Händler Frankreich:
Le Vins George Duboeuf, La Gare Romaneche-Thorins, La Chapelle-de-Guinchay

Artesa (former Codorniu Napa)
1345 Henry Road
Napa, CA 94559
Tel +1-707-224 16 68
Fax +1-707-224 16 72

Opening hours:
daily from 10.00-17.00

Tours:
11.00 and 14.00
(or by appointment)

Architect:
Domingo Triary, E. R. Bouligny

Wines:
Codorniu Napa methode champenoise sparkling wines, Artesa Chardonnay, Pinot Noir

Beringer Vineyards
2000 Main Street
St. Helena, CA 94574
Tel +1-707-963 71 15
Fax +1-707-963 17 35
e-mail info@bwecorp.com

Opening hours:
daily from 9.30-18.00 (May to Oct); 9.30-17.00 (Nov to Apr)

Tours every half hour
(no prior booking necessary)

Architect:
A. Schroepfer and others

Wines:
Private Reserve Napa Valley Cabernet Sauvignon, Private Reserve Napa Valley Chardonnay, Napa Valley Howell Mountain Merlot, Bancroft Ranch, Napa Valley Cabernet Sauvignon, Napa Valley Chardonnay, Napa Valley Fume' Blanc, Knights Valley Alluvium (proprietary blend), Knights Valley Alluvium Blanc (proprietary blend), North Coast Zinfandel, North Coast Pinot Noir, California Zinfandel Blush, California Collection Sauvignon Blanc, Chardonnay, Merlot and Cabernet Sauvignon

Wine merchant Germany:
Reidelmeister & Ulrichs GmbH, Bremen

Wine merchant France:
Le Vins George Duboeuf, La Gare Romaneche-Thorins, La Chapelle-de-Guinchay

Artesa (anciennement Codorniu Napa)
1345 Henry Road
Napa, CA 94559
Tel +1-707-224 16 68
Fax +1-707-224 16 72

Heures d'ouverture:
tous les jours de 10h00 à 17h00

Visites guidées:
11h00, 14h00 et sur rendez-vous

Architectes:
Domingo Triary et E. R. Bouligny

Vins:
Codorniu Napa méthode champenoise sparkling wines, Artesa chardonnay, pinot noir

Beringer Vineyards
2000 Main Street
St Helena, CA 94574
Tel +1-707-963 71 15
Fax +1-707-963 17 35
e-mail info@bwecorp.com

Heures d'ouverture:
de mai à octobre, tous les jours de 9h30 à 18h00
de novembre à avril, tous les jours de 9h30 à 17h00

Visites toutes les demi-heures, sans possibilité de réservation

Architecte:
A. Schroepfer, entre autres

Vins:
Private Reserve Napa Valley cabernet sauvignon, Private Reserve Napa Valley chardonnay, Napa Valley Howell Mountain Merlot, Bancroft Ranch, Napa Valley cabernet sauvignon, Napa Valley chardonnay, Napa Valley fumé blanc, Knights Valley alluvium (comppposition du propriétaire), Knights Valley alluvium blanc (composition du propriétaire), North Coast zinvandel, North Coast pinot noir, California zinvandel Blush, California Collection sauvignon blanc, chardonnay, merlot et cabernet sauvignon

Négociant en France:
Les vins George Duboeuf, La Gare Romaneche-Thorins, La Chapelle-de-Guinchay

Négociant en Allemagne:
Reidelmeister & Ulrichs GmbH, Brème

Clos Pegase
1060 Dunaweal Lane
Calistoga, CA 94515
Tel +1-707-942 49 81
Fax +1-707-942 49 93
e-mail clospegase@aol.com

Öffnungszeiten:
täglich 10.30 bis 17.00 Uhr

Führungen:
11.00 und 15.00 Uhr
Multi-Media Präsentation des
Besitzers Jan Shrem jeden 3.
Samstag im Monat um 14.00 Uhr
(außer Dezember und Januar)

Architekt: Michael Graves

Weine:
Merlot, Chardonnay Reserves,
Pinot Noir, Sauvignon Blanc,
Cabernet Franc, Vin Gris of
Merlot and Claret

Dominus
P.O. Box 3327
Yountville, CA 94599
Tel +1 707-944-8954
Fax +1 707 944-0547

das Weingut kann nicht
besichtigt werden!

Architekten:
Herzog & de Meuron

Weine:
Dominus, Napanook
(second wine)

Händler in Deutschland:
Segnitz & Co., Weye;
Schlumberger KG, Meckenheim

Clos Pegase
1060 Dunaweal Lane
Calistoga, CA 94515
Tel +1-707-942 49 81
Fax +1-707-942 49 93
e-mail clospegase@aol.com

Opening hours:
daily 10.30-17.00

Guided tours:
11.00 and 15.00
Multi-media presentation by
the owner, Jan Shrem every 3rd
Saturday of the month at 14.00
(exluding Dec and Jan)

Architect: Michael Graves

Wines:
Merlot, Chardonnay Reserves,
Pinot Noir, Sauvignon Blanc,
Cabernet Franc, Vin Gris of
Merlot and Claret

Dominus
P.O. Box 3327
Yountville, CA 94599
Tel +1 707-944-8954
Fax +1 707 944-0547

No visits possible

Architects:
Herzog & de Meuron

Wines:
Dominus, Napanook
(second wine)

Wine merchants Germany:
Segnitz & Co., Weye;
Schlumberger KG, Meckenheim

Clos Pegase
1060 Dunaweal Lane
Calistoga, CA 94515
Tel +1-707-942 49 81
Fax +1-707-942 49 93
e-mail clospegase@aol.com

Heures d'ouverture:
tous les jours de 10h30 à 17h00

Visites:
11h00 et 15h00
Présentation multi-média du
propriétaire Jan Shrem le troisième samedi de chaque mois à
14h00 (sauf en décembre et en
janvier)

Architecte: Michael Graves

Vins: merlot, chardonnay
reserves, pinot noir, sauvignon
blanc, cabernet franc, vin gris
of merlot and claret

Dominus
P.O. Box 3327
Yountville, CA 94599
Tel +1 707-944-8954
Fax +1 707 944-0547

On ne peut pas visiter le
domaine!

Architectes:
Herzog & de Meuron

Vins:
Dominus, Napanook (second vin)

Négociants en Allemagne:
Segnitz & Co., Weye;
Schlumberger KG, Meckenheim

Gérard Barthélémy

Jim Dine

Wayne Thiebaud

Far Niente
PO Box 327
Oakville, CA 94562
Tel   +1-707-944 28 61
Fax   +1-707-944 23 12
e-mail info@farniente.com

Öffnungszeiten:
täglich 8.00-16.30
Führung nur für Fachbesucher,
nicht offen für Publikum

Architekt:
Captain Hamden McIntyre

Weine:
Chardonnay, Cabernet
Sauvignon, Dolce (late harvest
dessert wine)

Händler Deutschland:
Weinhandlung Martin Apell,
Kassel

Händler Frankreich:
Domaines Ott, Clos Mireille, La
Londe Les Maures

Hess Collection
4411 Redwood Road
Napa, CA 94558
Tel   +1-707-255 11 44
Fax   +1-707-253 16 82
www.hesscollection.com

Öffnungszeiten:
täglich 10.00 bis 16.00 Uhr

Architekt:
Beat A.H. Jordi und
Richard MacRae

Weine:
Hess Collection Cabernet
Sauvignon Reserve, Hess
Collection Estate Cabernet
Sauvignon, Hess Collection Napa
Valley Merlot

Far Niente
PO Box 327
Oakville, CA 94562
Tel   +1-707-944 28 61
Fax   +1-707-944 23 12
e-mail info@farniente.com

Opening hours:
daily 8.00-16.30
Guided tours for business only,
not open to the general public

Architect:
Captain Hampten McIntyre

Wines:
Chardonnay, Cabernet
Sauvignon, Dolce (late harvest
dessert wine)

Wine merchant Germany:
Weinhandlung Martin Apell,
Kassel

Wine merchant France:
Domaines Ott, Clos Mireille, La
Londe Les Maures

Hess Collection
4411 Redwood Road
Napa, CA 94558
Tel   +1-707-255 11 44
Fax   +1-707-253 16 82
www.hesscollection.com

Opening hours:
daily from 10.00-16.00

Architect:
Beat A.H. Jordi and
Richard MacRae

Wines:
Hess Collection Cabernet
Sauvignon Reserve, Hess
Collection Estate Cabernet
Sauvignon, Hess Collection
Napa Valley Merlot

Far Niente
PO Box 327
Oakville, CA 94562
Tel   +1-707-944 28 61
Fax   +1-707-944 23 12
e-mail info@farniente.com

Heures d'ouverture:
tous les jours de 8h00 à 16h30
Visites guidées seulement pour
les professionnels

Architecte:
Captain Hamden McIntyre

Vins:
chardonnay, cabernet sauvignon, Dolce (vin doux de dessert)

Négociant en France: Domaines
Ott, Clos Mireille, La Londe Les
Maures

Négociant en Allemagne:
Weinhandlung Martin Apell,
Kassel

Hess Collection
4411 Redwood Road
Napa, CA 94558
Tel   +1-707-255 11 44
Fax   +1-707-253 16 82
www.hesscollection.com

Heures d'ouverture:
tous les jours de 10h00 à 16h00

Architecte:
Beat A.H. Jordi et
Richard MacRae

Vins:
Hess Collection cabernet sauvi-
gnon Reserve, Hess Collection
Estate cabernet sauvignon, Hess
Collection Napa Valley merlot

Opus One
7900 St. Helena Highway
Oakville, CA 94562
Tel +1-707-944 94 42
Fax +1-707-948 26 96

Guided tours by appointment

Architect: Scott Johnson

Opus One
7900 St. Helena Highway
Oakville, CA 94562
Tel +1-707-944 94 42
Fax +1-707-948 26 96

Führungen nach Vereinbarung

Architekt: Scott Johnson

Weine:
Opus One: A Bordeaux style red
wine comprised of Cabernet
Sauvignon, Merlot, Cabernet
Franc, Malbec and Petit Verdot.
(besonderer Jahrgang 1995)

Händler in Deutschland:
Reidelmeister & Ulrichs, Bremen

Händler in Frankreich:
Rothschild France Distribution,
Paris

Robert Mondavi
P.O. Box 106
Oakville, CA 94562
in Oakville gut vom Highway 26
erreichbar
Tel +1-707-226 13 95
Fax +1-707-968 21 66
e-mail info@robertmondavi.com

Öffnungszeiten:
täglich 9.00 bis 17.00 Uhr
(Mai bis Okt.); 9.30 bis 16.30
(Nov. bis April)

Architekt: Cliff May

Weine:
Robert Mondavi Costal, Robert
Mondavi Winery, Woodbridge, La
Famiglia

Händler Deutschland:
Hanseatisches Wein- und Sekt-
kontor (HAWESKO), Hamburg;
Alpina Burkhard Bovensiepen,
Buchloe; Hieber Wein, Anzing;
Weingut Heinz Schmitt, Leiwen;
Gute Weine, Bremen; Vereinigte
Weingutbesitzer, Koblenz; Gebr.
Schoemaker, Bremen; Veuve
Cliquot Import GmbH, Wies-
baden; Macha Weine & Feines,
Heidelberg; Mövenpick Weinland,
Dortmund

Händler Frankreich:
B.L.D. France, Paris

Wines:
Opus One: A Bordeaux style red
wine comprised of Cabernet
Sauvignon, Merlot, Cabernet
Franc, Malbec and Petit Verdot.
(special vintage 1995)

Wine merchant in Germany:
Reidelmeister & Ulrichs, Bremen

Wine merchant in France:
Rothschild France Distribution,
Paris

Robert Mondavi
P.O. Box 106
Oakville, CA 94562
Tel +1-707-226 13 95
Fax +1-707-968 21 66
e-mail info@robertmondavi.com

Opening hours:
daily from 9.00-17.00 (May to
Oct); 9.30-16.30 (Nov to Apr)

Architect: Cliff May

Wines:
Robert Mondavi Costal, Robert
Mondavi Winery, Woodbridge,
La Famiglia

Wine merchants Germany:
Hanseatisches Wein- und Sekt-
kontor (HAWESKO), Hamburg;
Alpina Burkhard Bovensiepen,
Buchloe; Hieber Wein, Anzing;
Weingut Heinz Schmitt, Leiwen;
Gute Weine, Bremen; Vereinigte
Weingutbesitzer, Koblenz; Gebr.
Schoemaker, Bremen; Veuve
Cliquot Import GmbH, Wiesba-
den; Macha Weine & Feines,
Heidelberg; Mövenpick Weinland,
Dortmund

Wine merchant France:
B.L.D. France, Paris

Opus One
7900 St. Helena Highway
Oakville, CA 94562
Tel +1-707-944 94 42
Fax +1-707-948 26 96

Visite sur rendez-vous

Architecte: Scott Johnson

Vins:
Opus One, un vin rouge de type
Bordeaux composé de cabernet
sauvignon, merlot, cabernet
franc, malbec et petit verdot
(année exceptionnelle 1995)

Négociant en France:
Rothschild France Distribution,
Paris

Négociant en Allemagne:
Reidelmeister & Ulrichs, Brème

Robert Mondavi
P.O. Box 106
Oakville, CA 94562
Tel +1-707-226 13 95
Fax +1-707-968 21 66
e-mail info@robertmondavi.com

Heures d'ouverture:
de mai à octobre, tous les jours
de 9h00 à 17h00
de novembre à avril, tous les
jours de 9h30 à 16h30

Architecte: Cliff May

Vins:
Robert Mondavi Costal, Robert
Mondavi Winery, Woodbridge, La
Famiglia

Négociants en Allemagne:
Hanseatisches Wein- und Sekt-
kontor (HAWESKO), Hambourg;
Alpina Burkhard Bovensiepen,
Buchloe; Hieber Wein, Anzing;
Weingut Heinz Schmitt, Leiwen;
Gute Weine, Brème; Vereinigte
Weingutbesitzer, Coblence; Gebr.
Schoemaker, Brème; Veuve
Cliquot Import GmbH, Wiesba-
den; Macha Weine & Feines,
Heidelberg; Mövenpick Weinland,
Dortmund

Négociant en France:
B.L.D. France, Paris

Robert Sinskey Vineyards
6320 Silverado Trail
Napa, California 94558
Tel   +1-707-944 90 90
Fax   +1-707-944 90 92
e-mail events@robertsinskey.com

Öffnungszeiten:
täglich 10.00 bis 16.30 Uhr

Führungen nach Vereinbarung

Architekt: Oscar Leidenfrost

Weine:
Chardonnay (Los Carneros of
Napa Valley), Stags Leap District
Clarent, Aries (Monterey, Pinot
Blanc), Cabernet Sauvignon (Los
Carneros of Napa Valley)

Sterling
1111 Dunaweal Lane
Castiloga, CA 94515
Zugang für Besucher nur über
eine Seilbahn möglich
Tel   +1 707 942 33 45
Fax   +1 707 942 34 67
e-mail concierge@sparkling.com

Öffnungszeiten:
10.30 und 16.30 Uhr

Architekt: Peter Newton

Weine:
Cabernet Sauvignon, Merlot,
Chardonnay, Sauvignon Blanc,
Pinot Noir

Händler Deutschland:
Reidelmeister & Ulrichs, Bremen

Robert Sinskey Vineyards
6320 Silverado Trail
Napa, California 94558
Tel   +1-707-944 90 90
Fax   +1-707-944 90 92
e-mail
events@robertsinskey.com

Opening hours:
daily from 10.00-16.30

Guided tours by appointment

Architect: Oscar Leidenfrost

Wines:
Chardonnay (Los Carneros of
Napa Valley), Stags Leap District
Clarent, Aries (Monterey, Pinot
Blanc), Cabernet Sauvignon (Los
Carneros of Napa Valley)

Sterling
1111 Dunaweal Lane
Castiloga, CA 94515
Access for visitors by cable car
only
Tel   +1 707 942 33 45
Fax   +1 707 942 34 67
e-mail concierge@sparkling.com

Opening hours: 10.30 and 16.30

Architect: Peter Newton

Wines:
Cabernet Sauvignon, Merlot,
Chardonnay, Sauvignon Blanc,
Pinot Noir

Wine merchant Germany:
Reidelmeister & Ulrichs, Bremen

Robert Sinskey Vineyards
6320 Silverado Trail
Napa, California 94558
Tel   +1-707-944 90 90
Fax   +1-707-944 90 92
e-mail
events@robertsinskey.com

Heures d'ouverture:
tous les jours de 10h00 à 16h00

Visites guidées sur rendez-vous

Architecte: Oscar Leidenfrost

Vins:
chardonnay (Los Carneros of
Napa Valley), Stags Leap District
Clarent, Aries (Monterey, pinot
blanc), cabernet sauvignon (Los
Carneros of Napa Valley)

Sterling
1111 Dunaweal Lane
Castiloga, CA 94515
Accès pour les visiteurs seule-
ment par téléphérique
Tel   +1 707 942 33 45
Fax   +1 707 942 34 67
e-mail concierge@sparkling.com

Heures d'ouverture:
tous les jours de 10h30 à 16h30

Architecte: Peter Newton

Vins:
cabernet sauvignon, merlot,
chardonnay, sauvignon blanc,
pinot noir

Négociant en Allemagne:
Reidelmeister & Ulrichs, Brème

Trefethen Vineyards
1160 Oak Knoll Avenue
Napa, CA 94558
Tel   +1-707-255 77 00
Fax   +1-707-255 07 93
e-mail
winery@trefethenwine.com

Öffnungszeiten:
täglich 10.00 bis 16.30 Uhr

Architekt:
Captain Hamden McIntyre

Weine:
Chardonnay, Dry Riesling,
Merlot, Cabernet Sauvignon,
Reserve Cabernet Sauvignon

Trefethen Vineyards
1160 Oak Knoll Avenue
Napa, CA 94558
Tel   +1-707-255 77 00
Fax   +1-707-255 07 93
e-mail winery@trefethen-
wine.com

Opening hours:
daily from 10.00-16.30

Architect:
Captain Hamden McIntyre

Wines:
Chardonnay, Dry Riesling,
Merlot, Cabernet Sauvignon,
Reserve Cabernet Sauvignon

Trefethen Vineyards
1160 Oak Knoll Avenue
Napa, CA 94558
Tel   +1-707-255 77 00
Fax   +1-707-255 07 93
e-mail
winery@trefethenwine.com

Heures d'ouverture:
tous les jours de 10h00 à 16h30

Architecte:
Captain Hamden McIntyre

Vins:
chardonnay, riesling sec,
merlot, cabernet sauvignon,
réserve cabernet sauvignon

Die Angaben stammen von den
jeweiligen Weingütern. Änderun-
gen und Irrtümer vorbehalten.
Stand November 1999

All specifications originate from
the corresponding vineyard. Any
changes and errors are subject to
alteration.
Status November 1999

Indications fournies par les viticulteurs - sauf erreur et sous ré-
serves de modifications.
Novembre 1999

Turnbull Wine Cellars
8210 St. Helena Highway
P.O. Box 29
Oakville, CA 94562
Tel   +1-707-963 58 39
Fax   +1-707-963 44 07

Öffnungszeiten:
täglich 10.00 bis 16.30 Uhr

Besichtigung nach Vereinbarung

Architekt: William Turnbull

Weine:
Cabernet Sauvignon, Merlot

Turnbull Wine Cellars
8210 St. Helena Highway
P.O. Box 29
Oakville, CA 94562
Tel   +1-707-963 58 39
Fax   +1-707-963 44 07

Opening hours:
daily from 10.00-16.30

Visits by appointment

Architect: William Turnbull

Wines:
Cabernet Sauvignon, Merlot

Turnball Wine Cellars
8210 St. Helena Highway
P.O. Box 29
Oakville, CA 94562
Tel   +1-707-963 58 39
Fax   +1-707-963 44 07

Heures d'ouverture:
tous les jours de 10h00 à 16h30

Visites guidées sur rendez-vous

Architecte: William Turnbull

Vins:
Cabernet Sauvignon, Merlot

Published February 2000 in the United States by
Gingko Press Inc.
5768 Paradise Drive, Suite J
Corte Madera, California 94925
415 924-9615 Tel
415 924-9608 Fax
gingko@linex.com

ISBN 1-58423-033-9

Published by arrangement with **av**edition
GmbH, Ludwigsburg

Imprint

Edited by Eva Wittwer and Petra Kiedaisch

English translation by Joanne Stead
French translation by Dominique Gauzin-Müller

Cover photograph by Olaf Gollnek
Opus One Vineyard

Design by **av**communication GmbH
Karin Skowronek

Lithography by **av**communication GmbH
Corinna Rieber

Production by **av**communication GmbH
Gunther Heeb

Printed by Leibfarth + Schwarz, Dettingen, Erms

Paper MultiArt Silk, 150g/qm

Printed in Germany

**Picture References/
Copyright**

All pictures from Olaf Gollnek
with exception of:

P. 40 + 43
Drawings: Château Cos
d'Estournel
P. 68 + 69
drawings in: Châteaux
Bourdeaux - Baukunst
und Weinbau, The German
Museum of Architecture,
Bern 1989
P. 83+84
Plans: Bernard, Marcel und
Jean-Marie Mazieres
P. 125
Trefethen Vineyards
P. 134, 135, 139
Michael Graves, in:
Michael Graves, Buildings
and Projects 1982-1998,
New York 1990
P. 195
Plans: Herzog & De Meuron